HISTORIC INNS of CORNWALL

Colin Gregory

Bossiney Books

*First published in 1986
by Bossiney Books
St Teath, Bodmin, Cornwall.
Typeset and printed in Great Britain
by Penwell Ltd., Parkwood, Callington, Cornwall.*

ISBN 0 948158 24 7

Plate Acknowledgements

*Cover photograph by Peter Keeling.
Ray Bishop: pages 5-11, 22-25, 31, 35, 54-58, 70, 72,
    76, 85-90, 95, 97, 101, 104, 106.
Author: pages 27, 29, 39, 41, 42, 43, 75, 77, 99.
Royal Institution of Cornwall: pages 19, 26, 33 &
    back cover.
Felicity Young: pages 30, 49, 67, 81.
Richard Isbell: pages 46, 51.
George Ellis: pages 66, 84.
Joan Cork: page 17.
David Wood: page 59.
John Lyne: page 68.
Cornish Photo News: page 78.
Paul Broadhurst: page 94.*

About the Author

Colin Gregory is a Cornishman who spent his early years less than a mile from the Bossiney Books base in North Cornwall.

Since 1972 he has worked for our regional daily newspaper *The Western Morning News* in Plymouth as deputy chief sub-editor, picture editor, and latterly, since moving to Truro, as district chief reporter. He attended Launceston College and then entered journalism with the *Cornish and Devon Post* at Launceston before continuing his education at the Cornwall Technical College and Bristol Polytechnic, after which he worked as an accountant before returning to newspapers.

It is as a newspaperman that he feels happiest, reporting on the triumphs, disasters, foibles, the fun and the sadness in Cornish life. His work as a journalist takes him all over Cornwall, and before he began *Historic Inns of Cornwall* he had first-hand knowledge of many of Cornwall's hostelries.

'A pint and a pasty is a journalist's working lunch,' he says. 'I have had a lot of fun in pubs, met many interesting people, made good friends, heard some excellent music and downed a few pints. I have a romantic view of pubs. Going out on a dark winter's night and seeing the lights in the distance is exciting. Outside it can be cold, wet and dismal—but inside there is a fire, people talking, a good evening in prospect.'

Colin loves Cornwall and things Cornish, especially Cornwall's history, characters of the past and present, the sea in summer and rugby in winter. His consuming hobby is collecting antique toys, which he thinks give an insight into the past and have some beauty in their construction and colour. He searches mainly for tin toys made before the First World War, and spends holidays and time off looking for them both in this country and Europe.

Historic Inns of Cornwall

To research fifty Historic Inns of Cornwall was a pleasure—not just because I had a pint in every one. Seeking the history of the buildings which for centuries have provided sustenance for travellers and locals, researching their existence and name, one generally stumbles across a whole unwritten area of social history.

Monks, murderers, wrestlers, writers, smugglers, national heroes, inventors, artists, marauders and even kings feature in their colourful past.

I was surprised at how little fact had been written down in the past about our Cornish hostelries. The churches and the local manor houses are generally well covered; the historians of the past tended to be the clergy or the well-to-do and they recorded what they thought was 'important'. Places where people gathered for pleasure were largely ignored.

It is worth making an attempt to put that right. Much of what has been written about pubs and inns has tended to be rumour or fanciful stories nurtured to give the premises some mystique. If I have not been comfortable about the provenance of a story I have tried to point this out. Some myths are dismissed, and in most cases the truth is more interesting.

The greatest problem I faced was to cut the number to the fifty required by this book. My original list of those worth tackling was twice as long, but settled on those I knew personally, those that made a good historical and geographical cross-section and those which I felt were significant in the locality or the county. That is not to say there are not other fascinating inns in Cornwall. There

Right: The King of Prussia at Fowey is probably named after Frederick the Great of Prussia.

4

KING of
PRUSSIA

certainly are, and I hope to be able to include them in a future publication. For easy reference the inns are arranged alphabetically according to location.

With regard to accurate information and history there was no-one who was able to offer me more help than Mr Leslie Douch, Curator of the Royal Institution of Cornwall at Truro. His excellent book *Old Cornish Inns* is the one to turn to for detailed information on the place of the hostelry in the social history of Cornwall. He kindly made his extensive research available to me—a gesture which gave my task a launching pad and was the backbone of my investigation.

Mr Douch deals with inns past and present, but as this book is aimed at the person who wants a helpful guide on places to visit I have included only those which are still open for business.

As landlords and landladies change over the years, I have in general not mentioned them even though they are excellent hosts. I have included them only when their connection has been so notable that it is part of the inn's history.

This is not a guide to the beer, wine or food offered in particular

6

Left: The Landlady at the Bull's Head, Callington.
Below: The Old Inn at Mullion—one of several thatched inns in Cornwall.

premises, but it is worth mentioning a welcome trend to more real ale in Cornish pubs, much of it produced locally by Devenish Brewery at Redruth, the St Austell Brewery, and some small brewers whose products are adding to the choice.

There is so much one finds out about Cornish history and customs in reading about the origin of our hostelries. They were the centres of sport and entertainment, some were held on three-life leases, reverting back to the owner on the death of the grandson of the original innkeeper.

Standards varied, from the bona fide inn, respectable enough for magistrates to hold their courts in, to the low drinking houses that were the haven of thieves and prostitutes in the last century. Most brewed their own beer, others such as the kettle-winks or kidley-winks simply provided hot-water for those who had a good supply of duty-free smuggled spirits.

Drinking houses abounded in the eighteenth and nineteenth centuries—at one stage there were over 100 in Truro alone. Numbers have decreased but the standards have risen. Let us hope they play their part in keeping customs alive, encourage good singing and traditional games, and provide us with a pleasant atmosphere in which to eat, drink and be merry for many years to come.

Right: Author, Colin Gregory.

8

BODMIN — *HOLE IN THE WALL*

One pub in Bodmin is a cosy and quaint hostelry in which to spend a friendly evening, but 200 years, or more, ago it was a virtual pit of misery and despair. The Hole in the Wall, in Crockwell Street, formerly known as Prison Lane, is the old Debtors' Prison. The low beams in the bars are now warm and welcoming, but it is not hard to imagine the dark, damp cells into which the wretched county debtors were thrown.

It is mentioned as a debtors' prison in 1750, at a time when the poor inmates had to pay for the doubtful privilege of being locked up.

In 1774 there were nineteen prisoners, and it is vividly described by John Howard, who travelled around the country to investigate

Right & Above: The Hole in the Wall at Bodmin,
formerly the Debtors' Prison.

Bass
Hole in the Wall
Free House
Bars Entrance
Hole in the Wall
FREE HOUSE
BASS ON DRAUGHT
Bass
Bass
Entrance to Bars
BODMIN
DEBTORS PRISON
1749-177

for his report on 'The State of the Prisons in England and Wales'. Howard said: 'It has a spacious backyard and stream running through it. Gatty the keeper pays £3-7-0d window tax.' The yard and stream are still there but, today, the landlord has to pay rather more 'window tax' in the form of rates.

In his report Howard also noticed that there was a 'Licence of late' which leads one to imagine that there had been a licence early in the eighteenth century for the purpose of the keepers' tap. The buildings certainly stretched back as far as 1700 for Howard notes they were 'out of repare' by 1777.

The Debtors' Prison and the House of Correction were put into disuse only two years later when the new Bodmin Prison was built. At one stage it was purchased by the Corporation of Bodmin for £1,000 in order to build a new market, but this never came to fruition and it was sold for £340—an early case of local government mis-spending! It became known as the Board Wine and Spirit Vaults by the 1870s, and as the Board Inn in the early years of this century.

In 1940 the name changed to 'Hole in the Wall' after the hole through which the family of a debtor would push food into the prison. It has always had a six-day licence, and no landlord has wished to apply to change it and lose his Sunday of rest.

BOLVENTOR — *JAMAICA INN*

'Ahead of her, on the crest, and to the left, was some sort of building, standing back from the road. She could see tall chimneys murky dim in the darkness. There was no other house, no other cottage.'

That was how Mary Yelland first saw Jamaica Inn in the opening chapter of Dame Daphne du Maurier's brilliant novel of that name, first published in 1936.

Thanks to Daphne du Maurier's superb story-telling Jamaica is now one of the most famous inns in Britain. It stands on the old coach road that ran from Launceston across the moor to Bodmin. The road of course, has changed dramatically since 1547 when the inn was built. Time was when travellers, across Bodmin Moor, had only tracks. Then, in 1769, a turnpike road was laid and coaches

*Jamaica Inn, which lent its name to Daphne du
Maurier's famous novel.*

rumbled across 'this howling wilderness' on their journeys from
London to Penzance—and back. Today the main A30 twists and
turns, plunges and rises across the landscape. But Jamaica Inn
itself somehow manages to generate a spirit of the past—especially
in winter: the cobbled courtyard, the great wooden door beneath the
porch leading into the lounge, a stone-flagged room with a log fire in
a gigantic grate; the swords, muskets, lanterns and ancient brass
hanging from the beams all combine to take you back in mood and
time.

The bars are based on the novel: Joss's Bar, named after the
coarse and brutal landlord Joss Merlyn, Mary's Bar, named after
the heroine from Helford, Smugglers Bar and Stable Bar.

Once a Temperance House, as it was when Daphne du Maurier
wrote her novel more than half a century ago, Jamaica has a
haunted reputation. Years ago, a stranger stood drinking a pot of
ale in the bar —a pot he was never to finish. Called outside, he put
down his half-empty tankard and disappeared into the dark Cornish
night. He never came back. They found his body out on the moor
next day, but they never discovered the identity of his
murderer. One landlord claimed to have heard the murdered man's
footsteps making their way along the passage to the bar—returning

to finish his tankard perhaps? A number of people also are reputed
to have seen a man sitting on the wall outside: a character who
never moved or spoke—and uncannily resembled the murdered
stranger.

Jamaica Inn was a posting house when the turnpike across the
moor was laid, and landlords would keep horses and provide
accommodation for travellers. In 1880 the premises were a temperance hotel, but on publication of Daphne du Maurier's book its
fortunes took another turn.

The name Jamaica Inn dates back to at least 1789, but the reason
for it is not known. An obvious explanation is that it sold Jamaica
rum, but historian H.L. Douch says there is a strong possibility
that someone considered its situation so unlike Jamaica that he
thought it worth the cynical comment.

BOSCASTLE — *COBWEB INN*

The Cobweb, a hundred yards back from Boscastle's magnificent
harbour and standing at the foot of the hill which climbs towards
Bude, only acquired a full licence in the 1940s. Yet it qualifies for
the label 'historic' for its connection with the drink and other trades
over many centuries.

Dating from the 1600s, this four-storey building was an off-licence
in the 1700s and for many years the warehouse and offices for a
general merchant. You could get a bag of coal, a pound of nails and a
bottle of scotch by visiting the Cobweb in the old days. Next door,
where there is now a pottery, was a bakery while the shop alongside
was a butcher's. So you could have picked up a loaf of crusty bread
and a round of beef on the same visit.

Highland whisky used to be bottled here in its general store days.
Among the bottles hanging in amongst the cobwebs from the beams
is one of the store's own brand, VOH (for Very Old Highland) and
another bottle marked 'H. Bowering, wine merchant, Boscastle'.

The present pub takes its name from those cobwebs which used to
fill the beams. They were there for a purpose, because the spiders
were in residence for centuries to kill off the wine flies which might
have ruined the stock.

The spiders have long gone, driven off by the smoke since the

*The Cobweb at Boscastle—when the building was a
warehouse spiders were encouraged to kill off the
wine flies.*

premises became a pub, while the cobwebs have largely come down
because of the heat and atmosphere. Those cobwebs which used to
be above the bar serving area had to come down—by order of the
public health inspectors.

In the Cobweb with its open fires, stone floors, wooden beams and
jolly company, it is not difficult to imagine those days when local
farmers and fishermen would sit down to a glass of wine, whisky or
beer from the barrel. The same fine pleasures are available today.
Even some of the chairs in the Cobweb have a history: one is a
hollowed elm tree and the other a carved buff chair which could be

15

as old as the building itself. The landlord since 1969 has also been a true piece of Cornwall—Ivor Bright, 'local born and bred'.

An especially interesting item at the Cobweb is a finely carved figure-head which came from a Swedish ship called *The Welm*. Back in 1890 she perished in a fierce gale on Black Rock, a few miles up the coast near Crackington Haven.

A curious tale links wines and spirits to the Non-Conformist chapel in Fore Street. A vessel, owned by Messrs Sloggatt and Rosevear, the Boscastle wine merchants, on a return voyage encountered a French privateer which attempted an ambush; but the Cornish captain, applying full sail, headed for home port. The Frenchman chased hard until both vessels were just off the entrance to Boscastle harbour. The French captain, thinking the Cornishman was heading for destruction, on the rocks, knowing nothing of the secret hidden harbour, sailed home to France without reward. Whereas on land the Boscastle wine merchants, in gratitude, contributed a generous sum of money for the enlargement of the teetotal chapel!

BOSCASTLE — *NAPOLEON INN*

The Napoleon Inn at Boscastle is almost in Paradise. That is not the dream of a regular customer sitting before its open fire with a welcome pint, but a fact. The Napoleon, which dates back to the sixteenth century, is a delightful whitewashed inn which clings to the steep hill that leads to the part of Boscastle which is called Paradise.

How it got its name, and which inn title came first—the Napoleon or the Wellington—is a matter of local argument. Tradition has it that it was used as a recruiting office for the Napoleonic wars and the landlord himself joined Wellington's ranks to go to Waterloo. On his return he was nicknamed 'The Napoleon Man' and christened his inn accordingly.

That is one story, but an interesting fact is that a landlord in the early part of the last century was called William Bone. In 1859 he was hauled before the local magistrates and fined for keeping a disorderly house and allowing gambling. As Napoleon Bonaparte was known in this country as 'Old Boney' one wonders if the nickname led to William Bone's pub getting its name.

Part of the inn is known as Boney's bar—so whether that is after the French Emperor or the Boscastle landlord we can only surmise. That the Napoleon and most of Boscastle is unspoilt is probably due to the fact that it was a Manor Estate up until 1946.

There were once eighteen public houses in Boscastle, with such names as The Jessie Logan, the Robin and the Sun Dial, and the village once had a lively fair. In 1886 Boscastle Fair became too lively, for the police had to be called to a disturbance outside the Napoleon. The village, especially its excellent public houses, has been known in more recent years for its local folk-singers.

One of the last of 'the old school' died in 1982. Charles Jose was 72, a farmer who had lived all his life in a stone farmhouse in the Valency Valley. He was known for his monologues and local songs, including one titled 'Boscastle Fair'. His cap still hangs beside his photograph in the public bar of the Napoleon, and often you will hear the new generation singing one of 'Charlie's songs'.

The Napoleon Inn at Boscastle.

BOSCASTLE — *WELLINGTON HOTEL*

You can approach Boscastle from various angles, probably the approach by boat is the most romantic, but as far as the land routes go, the journey in from Camelford is best. A glorious prospect over the Valency Valley and the Atlantic, from a height of some 800 feet: you suddenly, dramatically burst upon this view and begin the twisting descent into Boscastle itself.

At the foot of the Old Road stands the Wellington. Originally known as the Bos Castle Hotel, it was renamed Scott's Wellington on the Duke's death in 1852.

One of the oldest coaching inns along this North Cornish coast, the Wellington dates back more than three centuries, parts of the building even four centuries. Boscastle, in fact, depended on horse-drawn coaches until the early 1920s which makes the Wellington one of the last posting houses in Britain. A number of present-day residents can recall the coachman's horn, the clatter of hooves and the clink of harness as the coach rumbled down Fore Street into Dunn Street and the Old Hill depositing passengers in the yard.

An advertisement in *The Plymouth, Devonport and Stonehouse Herald*, dated 29 July 1849, read: 'The Albion Omnibus, with first-rate horses and driver, leaves Saltash every Wednesday at ten o'clock precisely, passes Callington and reaches Five Lanes twenty past three, where it remains for one hour, and finally reaches Boscastle with Mail Coach regularity at seven o'clock. Fares, whole distances, 4s 6d inside, 3s 4½d outside.'

Substantially rebuilt in 1853, the Wellington today is a scheduled historic building. If you pay a visit, try to see the exquisite hanging oil lamps, which originally hung in St Juliot Church, installed by Hardy himself. Other interesting features are the collection of etchings and prints concerning the Duke of Wellington and the four stained-glass windows in the long bar—these came from another Cornish coaching inn, Olivers' Royal Hotel at Bodmin. They were made in 1846 to commemorate Queen Victoria's visit to the county town, each window being in the shape of a quarter of the Royal Standard.

Unfortunately there is no evidence to indicate a visit by the General 'with his hooked nose and piercing eye', but in the 1870s, a

The Wellington at Boscastle—one of the last posting houses in Britain.

royal party stayed at the hotel which, it is believed, included Edward VII and a lady friend.

Another eminent visitor in the last century was Sir Henry Irving, the first actor to be knighted. Somerset-born, Irving spent most of his childhood in West Cornwall, and later, in an interview with Sir Arthur Quiller-Couch, attributed his stamina to 'the free and open and healthy years' he had enjoyed in the south-west. A chair, used by Irving in some of his London productions, was made of woodwork from Minster Church removed during its restoration when timber changed hands for less than £1 a ton.

Irving was greatly interested in the reputed magical powers of a certain Boscastle woman—believed to be a witch—so much so that

19

*The Falcon Hotel at Bude around 1900—its coaches
ran to Clovelly, Bideford, Boscastle, Tintagel and
Newquay.*

he gave her an allowance, paid quarterly by the wife of the Boscastle
doctor. A string of misfortunes robbed the famous actor-manager of
most of his money in the 1890s, and it is possible that he may have
been hoping to use her powers to unwind the bad spell.

BUDE — *FALCON HOTEL and BRENDON ARMS*

The Falcon, standing watch over the Bude Canal, is said to be the
oldest coaching house in North Cornwall and until recent years a
beautiful old coach stood on the hotel lawns. Bude started as a
seaport for the canal which once stretched thirty miles inland to
Launceston, and was busy in the 1820s with barges carrying
seasand which was used to add minerals to farm soil.

The town's reputation as a resort grew later, especially with the
advent of the railway, now sadly gone, and the reputation and
fortune of the Falcon grew with it. Way back in 1826 Bude was
proud to boast that it had received 500 visitors during the season.
'The accommodation afforded the company has been beyond all
preceding years, especially since the reopening of the Falcon', a local

newspaper reported glowingly. Nowadays, 500 people on the resort's spacious beaches on one summer afternoon would be regarded as quiet.

The Falcon was the headquarters of the large four-horse coaches which provided regular services between Westcountry towns. Some of the old harnesses and coach wheels are displayed in the bar, together with photographs showing Bude's maritime past. The Brendon Arms is named after the family which owned and ran the Falcon for 100 years until recent times. Just across the canal from the Falcon and the Brendon Arms is the little castle which was built in the 1830s by Sir Goldsworthy Gurney, inventor of the 'Bude Light', an oil lamp which was designed for lighthouses. He also built a steam-powered coach which must have been viewed with some scepticism by the stable staff at the Falcon.

The Falcon has had a number of famous guests, including Alfred, Lord Tennyson, who stayed there in 1826. Neither Tennyson nor those gentle souls who came for bracing seaside strolls from the Falcon at that time could have envisaged the little port of Bude becoming 'Britain's Bondi'.

CALLINGTON — *BULL'S HEAD INN*

The Bull's Head, Callington's oldest public house, has seen much of the town's history. It stands on the corner opposite the fifteenth-century church, and was itself built at about the same time. Deeds for the land on which it stands go back even farther. Old maps of the town show it standing in the area where the market used to be held. In the middle of the road was a property known as Island House, while opposite on Fore Street stood the New Inn, now no longer a public house. The property once belonged to a prominent local family, the Corytons. John Coryton, the first baronet, became one of Callington's MPs and was a well-known Tory.

It is because of this link that the Bull's Head would host the Tory supporters during the times of eighteenth-century elections while the New Inn across the road would be full of Whigs. Callington, like many similar towns in Cornwall, has always been a hot bed of politics. It had two MPs up to the time of the 1832 Reform Act when it lost its Borough status and became part of the East

Cornwall constituency. The Tory Corytons held the seat in the family for over seventy years, until it passed to the Whigs. Election time was always exciting in Callington—with the end result revelry or recrimination in the Bull's Head—depending on which side won.

Its age can be judged by an advertisement of 1749. Even then it was described as 'an ancient Inn'. There was a sale of all furniture 'including very good beds (mostly new) looking glasses etc.' It joined the age of transport in 1768 when the landlord announced post chaises for hire. In the 1920s a photograph of the Bull's Head advertised 'stabling and lock-up garage'. The Bull's Head had entered the age of the motor car but it still has the atmosphere of the post chaise.

CALLINGTON — *THE OLD CLINK*

Some people may dream of being locked in a public house, but at 'The Old Clink' in Callington, many years ago, they would have found the experience most uncomfortable. The name, 'The Old Clink', leaves little to the imagination. The inn is, in fact, just across the road, in the narrowest part of Callington main street, from the Old Lock-up which was built in 1851. The inn itself is much older, thought to be sixteenth-century or seventeenth-century.

It was first known as the Red Lion, then the Commercial, and in the late sixties its name was changed to 'The Old Clink' because of its proximity to the prison which was put up at a cost of sixty pounds in the middle of the last century. The Old Clink had two lock-up cells for drunks and vagrants, but by the turn of the century wrong-doers found themselves a little way up the road instead of repenting their actions in these cramped cells. By then they were taken to the Victorian Police Station in Tavistock Road.

The present-day public house has quite a past, even without its connections with the forbidding clang of the cell door. It was a highly esteemed coaching inn and one has only to look at the yard at the rear to see that it was once a busy stopping place for thirsty and hungry travellers. A restaurant now occupies the stables. The floor is still of stone cobbled sets and the original horse troughs now

Left: The Bull's Head at Callington.

*The Old Clink at Callington named after the Lock-up
built opposite in 1851.*

make five plant holders. The restaurant kitchen was once the hay-
loft—the fodder is much more appetising now.

Underneath the inn is a cellar which has a bricked-up door. This is
believed to lead to a tunnel which goes through to the prison across
the road. The Old Clink is said to have a ghost—a woman who looks
through a window into the bar. Many a husband has probably seen
this after spending too long enjoying the hospitality of the inn!

CREMYLL, MILLBROOK — *EDGCUMBE ARMS*

The Edgcumbe Arms stands at the water's edge at Cremyll, looking
across the Hamoaze, that stretch of river and sea, to Devonport and
Plymouth. Over the water, in Devon, are the Royal Navy's Victual-

ling Yard and Her Majesty's Dockyard. The Cremyll ferry will take passengers across and bring them back, just in time for a drink at the Edgcumbe Arms. The inn is near the entrance to the Mount Edgcumbe Country Park, which is itself worth the trip down to this tip of Cornwall which used to be part of Devon.

The first records of a passage house on the spot are in 1730, although parts of the building may be a little earlier. The ferry used to run from Barnpool, a short distance seawards, but moved to Cremyll in 1720 and now crosses to Admiral's Hard. Much of what you see on the other side was built by French prisoners during the Napoleonic Wars. Newspapers first mention the inn, then known as the Passage House, in 1762. Ralph Banks, late steward to Commodore Edgcumbe, announced opening a commodious inn with six warm and well fitted-up lodging rooms. There was also a large stable and coach house.

Thirty years later another landlord took over, announcing: 'A whiskey and horse may be had for pleasure in viewing the Beauties of Mount Edgcumbe. A Bathing Machine for all seasons.' Later its

Children wait outside the Edgcumbe Arms for the Cremyll ferry to take them across to Plymouth.

The Greenbank Hotel, Falmouth, as it was around 1900 . . .

name was changed to the Ferry House and by 1852 to the Mount Edgcumbe Arms. The inn certainly had a fine reputation. A Mrs Topsham, writing of her six-week tour in 1796, said: '. . . an excellent house, good beds, good victuals of all sorts, fish in the greatest perfection . . . It is the next best thing to being in one's house, everything was so comfortable.' A few days later she described another inn as 'a very bad house'. Looking back to the Ferry Inn she remarked:'Before I quit this part of the world I must say that Mr and Mrs Phillips are the most civil attentive people that I ever knew, and very reasonable in their charges and everything of the very best.' High praise indeed, and the reputation has been continued down the years.

FALMOUTH — *GREENBANK HOTEL*

What was once a simple inn, beside a ferry crossing, has grown to become a superb hotel—with the help of famous characters from both fiction and history along the way. Greenbank is an apt name

The Greenbank Hotel as it is today.

for the birthplace of a toad, mole and rat, for it is here that the characters of *Wind in the Willows* evolved. Kenneth Grahame's classic began as a series of letters sent to his son. The first two were written at the Greenbank while Grahame was a guest in May 1907. They are reproduced for display at the hotel and begin 'My darling mouse' and 'My dearest mouse'. Grahame, after a delightful description of a birthday present, asks his son, 'Have you heard about Toad?' He then goes on to tell a story. Florence Nightingale stayed at the hotel a month before Grahame, one of many famous people who admired the views of the bay, Pendennis and St Mawes Castles, and Falmouth harbour from the window of the Greenbank.

The original inn on the site, known in 1785 as The Ship, grew up with the ferry service to Flushing. The 'service' was debatable as operators, who were usually also the innkeepers, would delay the crossings so that the passengers would drink more. In 1809 the landlord of The Ship was declared bankrupt, so the new landlord, who advertised that he hoped 'by strict attention to merit a share of the public favours' changed the name to The King's Arms. It was soon changed to the Commercial and Packet before being called the

Greenbank because of its location.

It was a well-known coaching inn. In 1815 the landlord announced that he would cut the cost of travel because of a reduction in the price of forage. In 1819 the Greenbank announced: 'The Lord Exmouth Subscription Coach leaves the hotel every morning for Plymouth, Exeter, London, Bath and Bristol. Neat post, with careful drivers, to any part of England.'

The Greenbank is proud of its history and has on display a fine collection of letters, guest registers, and models of boats with local associations.

FIVE LANES — *KINGS HEAD HOTEL*

Bodmin Moor is a majestic but wild stretch of Cornwall. It must have presented a hard journey for the traveller of old.

The sight of oil lamps burning in an inn, the warmth of the fire, and thought of a welcoming glass of ale or porter would have cheered the final stage of any trek across the moor. It is not surprising that an inn at Five Lanes, on the northern side of that great moor and beside the old main route to London from Cornwall, was so popular.

Built in 1623 it is said to have been occupied by both factions of the Civil War just twenty years later. The Kings Head was a coaching inn when its now more famous neighbour, Jamaica Inn, simply catered for the occasional thirsty traveller and a few moorland farmers.

It has not always had the same name. In 1771 it was known as the Indian Queen, twelve years later as the London Inn, and in 1795 as the Five Lanes Inn. Its attraction was illustrated when a new landlord announced he was taking over. He proclaimed in a newspaper advertisement: 'Five Lanes cannot be exceeded in point of situation for rendering speed and convenience by breaking the long stages, being thirteen miles east of Bodmin and twelve miles west of Lifton where the White Horse Inn furnishes neat carriages, able horses and very good accommodation.'

Not long after the inn was itself offering two post chaises and six chaises horses. In 1804, when it was known as the Five Lanes Inn, it was sold. An advertisement revealed that an annual fair or revel

A model of the **Mercury,** *a Falmouth packet ship sailing in the 1790s, on display at the Greenbank Hotel.*

held at the rear of the inn was very profitable to the landlord.

A market is held just behind the inn even now, on Wednesdays, and the farmers, who come in for refreshment and to continue their business of buying and selling cattle, sheep and horses, still bring some profit.

A proprietor, Mr John Broad, was in residence for 44 years at the beginning of the nineteenth century. His wife carried it on until her

The Kings Head at Five Lanes on the edge of Bodmin Moor.

death and when it was let in 1859 the *West Briton* newspaper said: 'This Inn was formerly kept by the late Mrs Broad by whom a considerable fortune was realised.'

The Kings Head is said to have a ghost, Peggy Bray, who hanged herself in the inn after she was deserted by a man. He is supposed to have left her to follow John Wesley in the mid eighteenth century.

FOWEY — *KING OF PRUSSIA HOTEL*

The centre of Fowey's maritime activity has been Town Quay. It is still very busy, but now cars park where the Bronze Age tin traders, missionaries, and saints first set foot in England. Just back from the quay, the old inn known as the King of Prussia has stood for more than two hundred years, and under its granite columns there used to be a busy buttermarket. Local tradition has it that the public house is named after John Carter, the smuggler from West Cornwall whose derring-do in beating the customs men in the late eighteenth century, made him a local folk hero.

He dubbed himself the 'King of Prussia' when playing soldiers as a boy, having heard of the exploits of Frederick the Great of Prussia during the Seven Years War. However, the newspaper, *The Sherborne Mercury*, reports a fire at the King of Prussia in 1765, yet John Carter is not supposed to have entered the smuggling trade seriously until five years later. The truth of the matter seems to be that the King of Prussia at Fowey, like many other inns at the time, was named after Frederick the Great, whose spectacular

The King of Prussia has stood for more than 200 years just back from Town Quay at Fowey.

victories against the French and Austrians from 1756-1763 made him a hero in this country.

Truro Museum Curator, Leslie Douch, in his *Old Cornish Inns* agrees, saying, 'If Fowey wished to dethrone Frederick the Great, it had enough notorious smugglers of its own to commemorate.' John Carter, the self-styled smuggler king, was operating up to 1807 and became so well-known that his home 'Bessy's Cove' in Mount's Bay was named Prussia Cove. The fact that the inn changed its allegiance from a monarch to a smuggler probably dates back to the First World War, when, naturally, all things German were despised. With two such famous men associated with it, perhaps it should now be called 'The Kings of Prussia'.

FOWEY — *LUGGER INN*

Fowey has a seafaring history over many centuries, be it in fishing, piracy or in the service of the monarch, so it is not suprising so many of the inns have names such as The Ship, the Safe Harbour, and the Lugger. Life in this charming Cornish seaport was so ably recorded, with some journalistic licence, in the books of Sir Arthur Quiller-Couch, known as 'Q', and if you walk along Fowey's narrow streets his stories come alive.

The Lugger Inn was already an ancient inn when 'Q' began to record the comings and goings of the townsfolk of his beloved 'Troy Town'.

As far back as the sixteenth century there was a building on this site in Fore Street. This may have provided the foundations of the Lugger, which from 1787 to 1806 was the meeting place for the Court Leet. Newspapers of that time record the Manor Court 'held at the house known by the sign of The Lugger'. The Lugger has been renovated as was necessary for a thriving inn over several centuries, both inside and out. Upstairs there was a plaque of 1633 which commemorated a plaster ceiling of that date, but this has been replaced by a metal sign.

The Lugger fits so well into the street scene. A little further along the road is the Globe Posting House; this was the Globe Inn in

Right: The Lugger Inn at Fowey in the 1890s.

coaching days. Beyond the Globe is one of the most interesting working houses in Fowey, the Noah's Ark. This dates back to the sixteenth century, or farther, and is now an art shop and museum.

The social history of Fowey has been turbulent for such a small town, which was the scene of battles between Royalists and Parliamentarians at nearby Castle Dore. Down the road by the church there was an old public house called the Rose and Crown. It was closed down in 1810 when William Wyatt, the landlord, murdered a Jewish moneylender Isaiah Valentine. Wyatt was subsequently hanged at Bodmin. No-one wanted to buy the Rose and Crown and the premises were incorporated in the churchyard.

For a detailed and knowledgeable guide through the narrow streets and perpendicular hills of Fowey you should seek out a copy of the Fowey History Group's excellent publication: *Looking at Fowey.*

FOWEY — *THE SHIP INN*

The front of this lovely old tavern somehow resembles the stern of one of those old-time men o' war. The building was once the town house of a wealthy local merchant family, the Rashleighs, but it became an inn before 1700. Writings of 1896 record that the name of a gallant little ship, the *Frances of Fowey*, which went to America with Frobisher in the late 1500s, had been preserved in the name of The Ship Hotel. Its quaint front was looking down on passers-by in much the same way as it did two hundred years before.

In remembrance and memory of the old ship, the *Frances*, local people had a figure of the vessel, about five feet long, made by a ship's carpenter and this was hung from the roof of the hotel. During restoration of The Ship in 1891 a large swinging signboard was discovered in the attic. One side showed an English sloop engaged with a French frigate, the other a full rigged East Indiaman. The Ship has had extensive alterations through the centuries, but it still retains a fine ceiling from the early days and an

34

inscription over one of the fireplaces which reads 'John Rashleigh —
Alice Rashleigh 1570'.

The stables of The Ship were a little further up Lostwithiel Street,
and there are mentions in old newspapers of neighbours
complaining about the smell of horse manure.

Its age can be gauged by an advertisement in the *Sherborne
Mercury* of 1758, when it was described as 'an inn of the chiefest
note' which had been in operation for a long period. Fowey must
have been alert to the holiday trade a long time ago, for in 1802 the
landlord of The Ship built a 'commodious bathing machine' on a
nearby beach.

In 1809 Lord Grenville's Manor Court was held at The Ship, and

in the 1860s inhabitants of the inn figured in court cases which give us a picture of life at the time. In August, 1860, the landlord John Sparnall was fined for using an unlicensed stage carriage, and the next month a boy employed by him was put in the stocks for theft. In 1863 the new landlord, John Frost, was fined for driving an un-licensed carriage at over four miles per hour—a case of being 'reck-less behind the reins'.

HELFORD PASSAGE — *FERRY BOAT INN*

Many of the county's most famous inns originated as passage houses, where people could stop for a drink while waiting for a ferry to take them across one of Cornwall's numerous creeks. The Ferry Boat, formerly called the Passage Inn faces the water at Helford Passage, between Mawnan Smith and Constantine, and by all accounts had the most troublesome bunch of ferrymen in all Cornwall. The ferry operators also invariably ran the passage house at either side of the water, so it was to their advantage to keep the travellers waiting to encourage them to spend more on drinks. The boatmen were also inveterate tipplers themselves.

A farmer from nearby Budock was so incensed at being kept waiting at Helford Passage that he sprang into verse:

> *Of all ye mortals here below*
> *Your drunken boatmen are the worst I know,*
> *I'm here detained, tho' against my will*
> *While these sad fellows sit and drink their fill.*
> *Oh Jove! to my request let this be given,*
> *That these same boatmen ne'er see hell nor heaven,*
> *But with old Charon ever tug the oar*
> *And neither taste nor swallow one drop more.*

Over eighty years later the situation did not seem to have improved. Miss Fox, of Penjerrick, was so disgusted at the delays caused by the 'indolence of boatmen' that she had a wooden house built on the Lizard side of the water so that passengers could wait in shelter rather than walk all the way around Gweek or be forced to spend time and money in the public house on that side. The landlord of the Ferry Boat at that time certainly had little respect for authority. His licence was adjourned for being impertinent to the magistrate when charged with keeping illegal Sunday hours.

Nowadays the ferrymen, who operate from Good Friday to the end of October, are a more prompt and sober band. The inn itself is also different as it was rebuilt from an old cottage in the 1920s. It has had many famous guests. Actor David Niven spent a 'delayed honeymoon' here in 1945 and shortly before his death wrote of his memories of standing in the river at Helford Passage receiving oysters from a passing boatman.

HELSTON — *ANGEL HOTEL*

There can be very few inns with a well in the lounge, but the Angel Hotel at Helston has one. The well, in which the water level rises and falls according to the rainfall, is forty feet deep and is now lit up

so that customers can see the bottom. In the old days it would have been as useful as having water on tap, because this part of the hotel used to be the kitchen. It is easy to imagine the 'downstairs' staff drawing up the water in wooden buckets.

The well is not the only unusual feature of this ancient building, which fits so well into Coinagehall Street in this attractive old town. The dining room has the original Minstrel's Gallery, where musicians would have entertained the guests. A great deal of old furniture has survived in the hotel to preserve the feel of a very special building. A stone in the wall is said to be a relic of the Archangel Michael's battle with the Devil. It was called the Hell-Stone, reputed to be the lid of Hell and was on display in the rear yard intact until 1783 when it was broken up and built into a side wall of the hotel. Superstition has it that any woman living in the Angel would suffer some sort of tragedy because of the presence of the Hell-Stone.

The Angel, built in the sixteenth century, was once the town house of the Godolphins, a famous old Cornish family. Tax and excise were later paid at the back of the house and it became a temporary gaol for smugglers before becoming an hotel and posting house. In 1756 it was let as 'a house of great business and good accommodation'. It also had a cock-pit, the scene of bloody battles between birds which seemed to appeal to the 'sporting' men of those days—now thankfully illegal.

Its role as a posting house is shown in an advertisement of 1783 which states that the landlord sacked an ostler for ill-treating a customer's horse. As well as stating that he would henceforth take 'particular' care in future about whom he employed as ostler, the

Below: The Angel Hotel at Helston, once the town house of the Godolphin family. Left: Furry Day—last century the day would end with dancing at the Angel.

landlord announced improvements to the hotel including 'two very elegant dining rooms, three lodging rooms and a new sixteen-stall stable'.

By 1861 the posting business was advertised for sale as 'the oldest in Cornwall', with eight horses and nine carriages including a hearse. At that time the mail coach arrived twice daily from Camborne and two-horse omnibuses ran to and from nearby towns.

It was in the Godolphin family until 1785. On the death of the last member of the family in 1785 it passed to the Earl of Godolphin's son-in-law, the fourth Duke of Leeds, whose wife had died. It was sold by the Leeds family for the first time in 1921. In the last century the famous Helston Furry Day would end with dancing at the Angel. Now the huge throng would not get inside the ballroom, but the Angel still plays its part in this ancient custom.

HELSTON — *THE BLUE ANCHOR*

The Blue Anchor needs little introduction to lovers of real ale, because its home-brewed beer, known as 'Spingo' is famous in its own right. The small brewery at the rear of The Blue Anchor is probably the oldest brewery in the British Isles. Two or three times a week in the winter, and up to six times weekly in summer the head brewer does his stuff and comes up with five different strengths and flavours. The 'secret ingredient' is said to be water from the well at the rear. Extra Special, with a specific gravity of 1070, is described as 'a strong headbanger' while the mild, at 1040, is a fairly recent introduction. The Special, Best Bitter and Medium are among the most popular, and the wisest choice for those who want flavour and strength without being a 'headbanger'.

Pilgrims on their way to St Michael's Mount would have stopped at Helston. The building started life as a monks' rest house about the year 1400, and when the monasteries were dissolved it became a tavern. The skittle alley at the rear was a favourite rendezvous for the local gentry, while the bar was frequented by the tin miners. It is said that company clerks paid out the miners' wages, as low as five shillings a week, at The Blue Anchor. The original count house,

Right: The Blue Anchor at Helston.

40

The Blue Anchor
Spingo
skittle   alley

the financial headquarters of the nearby miners, was known as the
Coinagehall, and the street where you will find The Blue Anchor is
named after it.

There have been some strange deaths at The Blue Anchor. In
1717 the landlord James James is said to have been stabbed to
death after intervening in a scuffle between two wayfarers. They
were both hanged at Bodmin. In 1828 a man died after falling down
the well. A former landlord, Geoff Richards, remembers a man who
used to take his hat off by the well and say, 'Father drowned here.'
Later, in 1849, a man committed suicide by hanging from one of the
beams in the skittle alley. Local talk has it that his depression was
caused by his wife continually nagging him about playing the game,
saying, 'You'll die in that skittle alley.'

*Below: The Blue Anchor is famous for 'Spingo', its
home-brewed beer.*

HESSENFORD — *COPLEY ARMS*

Hessenford, on the A387 road from Looe to Plymouth, lies in the wooded Seaton valley and was a coaching stop into Cornwall after St Germans, which had the chief church in the county before the building of Truro Cathedral in the 1880s. The Copley Arms, which stands beside the river and has part of its car park on the opposite bank, is said to have been a public house since the 1400s. It takes its name from the surrounding estate, and the slate cottages of the village were built for the workers.

At one time there were two public houses in Hessenford. The Copley Arms was the name of premises which were on the other side of the road while the present inn was called the Cornish Arms. There was also a beerhouse in the eighteenth century with the most obvious of names—The Mug and Glass. The village was a self-sufficient unit, with a cobbler who operated from the rear of the inn, a blacksmith and a mill for grinding corn. A cattle fair used to be held on the meadow across the bridge between the Copley Arms and the mill, with a fine dinner at the inn in the evening to mark the occasion.

A saw mill also operated in this wooded valley, and the busy village life was completed by a church and chapel. The authorities during the eighteenth century frowned on the small alehouses of the time. St Germans vestry books of 1783 show that people known, or reputed to keep 'brandy shops or idle tippling houses' had their parish pay suspended.

Hessenford and the Copley Arms is worth a stop. One regular visitor thinks there was an abbey nearby, pillaged by the Normans and Saxons, and that the valuables were hidden. So, there could be gold or silver chalices in them thar hills!

KILKHAMPTON — *LONDON INN*

Like so many inns in olden times the London Inn was church property. Also, as with many old drinking houses, it is difficult to establish when the business started, but some idea of the age of the inn can be gleaned from writings of 1788 which described it as 'from time immemorial the London Inn'. Six years earlier a new landlord had opened with much aplomb, and his advertisement in the *Exeter Flying Post* at the time is worth repeating for its descriptive charm so typical of the period. 'He has laid in, and is resolved to keep, an assortment of the best liquors, genuine in their kinds, and will exert his endeavours to render every other accommodation agreeable. With this, together with a perseverance in, and submissive attention to his business, he hopes to merit their countenance and support.'

Some years later the London Inn was let by the church to the wonderfully-named 'People's Refreshment House Association'. The London Inn, even in days when there were a number of similar establishments in this North Cornish village, had some cachet of respectability above the rest. Church meetings, presided over by the vicar were held there to deal with the relief of the poor. An ancient minute book shows the amount paid to the poor and sick, together with something for those who attended when death comes. Payment in this respect was for 'stretching him out'. The village Friendly Society also used to hold their meetings at the London Inn. Following Divine Service at the parish church they would march in procession through the village behind the Morwenstow Brass Band.

*The London Inn at Kilkhampton, its name indicating
that it was on a coaching route to the capital.*

The name, London Inn, indicates that it was on a coaching route to
the capital. There are stables to the rear of the inn, and the four-feet
thick cob walls and ships' timbers used in the construction of the
rear part of the building indicate it is much older than the front,
said to have been added a mere 300 years ago.

LANREATH — *PUNCH BOWL INN*

The charming village of Lanreath, with its picturesque cottages,
manor house and Norman church, has an inn with plenty of history
and character. To find it you travel down a little road for a short
distance, leaving the B3359 that links Looe to the main St Austell
to Liskeard route.

Lanreath was once on the busy main route from Fowey to
Plymouth, via the Bodinnick Ferry, but now the bulk of traffic
passes it by and the village is a place where people can live in peace

RAC
Hotel
THE FAMOUS OLD
Punch Bowl Inn
AND STABLE RESTAURANT
Worthington
'E'
PUNCH BOWL INN
FREE HOUSE
AA

*Left: The Punch Bowl Inn at Lanreath where the inn
sign (above) was designed by Augustus John.*

and enjoy a quiet pint. When Fowey was a bustling port in the
1700s, full of sailing ships, coaches would have stopped at the
Punch Bowl for refreshment for both passengers and horses.
Standing opposite the parish church it has long been well-known for
its food and drink and has always been a central part of village life,
serving as a courthouse in the times when it was a much busier
village. Many of the village men would have been employed in the
nearby mines, while before mechanisation scores of workers,
including women and children, were on the land. The seventeenth
century manor house in the village, Court, would have employed
many people for milking, harvesting and helping around the farm.
There were enough people living around to support two other public
houses, the Trecan Gate Inn and the White Horse, both of which
have long disappeared.

The Visitors' Kitchen—bars have always been known as kitchens at the Punch Bowl—served as the courthouse. This used to be the main bar or kitchen, but the inn has been extended since through the purchase of adjoining cottages and also includes a 'Farmers' Kitchen'. The inn sign is also interesting as it was designed in the 1950s by the painter Augustus John. He was a friend of the landlord and a frequent visitor. One family kept the Punch Bowl for close on 200 years. They were the Leans who, up to 1867, ran two establishments. Eventually, Noah Lean, the father, who had bought the Punch Bowl from Lieutenant General F.W. Buller, purchased the White Horse from his son for £65 and the two were merged.

Like many pubs the Punch Bowl has a ghost, but this one is sealed inside a clome oven in the lounge! The story, which you can read in the Farm Museum opposite the inn, concerns an aged vicar of Lanreath, his young and beautiful wife, and a new curate. According to legend the curate and the wife fell in love, and one night, after they had all dined, the vicar fell down the steps of his wine cellar and died. The following day a black cockerel appeared in the village and attacked everyone. People said it was the vicar's ghost, and no-one could catch it. Eventually it flew through the open window of the Punch Bowl where, with great presence of mind, the kitchen maid shut it in the clome oven. A mason was called to cement the door, so there, to this day, is the spirit of the Rector of Lanreath.

LAUNCESTON — *WHITE HART HOTEL*

The White Hart is the oldest hotel in Launceston, and its granite doorway, which came from the Old Priory at Newport, is of even greater antiquity. Standing proudly in the Square of this ancient capital of Cornwall the White Hart faces the Norman Castle which was constructed in the early years after the Conquest of 1066. Launceston was the centre of Cornish administration and the medieval castle presided over the town as the place where officials lived, rents were paid and punishment meted out.

Right: The doorway of the White Hart at Launceston,
brought from the Old Priory at Newport.

48

The priory would have been built just after the Conquest but after the Dissolution of the Monasteries in the sixteenth century it was left derelict. It soon became the source of some free building stone and it is almost certain a doorway was carried up the hill to its present position as the entrance to the White Hart.

The hotel was the centre of the town's social activities. Entries for the Launceston Races on St Stephen's Down in 1755 were received at the White Hart; cockfighting 'between the gentlemen of Devon and Cornwall' took place alongside the hotel. As a centre of justice, Launceston was the home of the Assizes. People came to judge and be judged, to watch and in some cases, to gloat over the free entertainment. John Pearse, the landlord of the White Hart in 1767, was keen to solicit business. He advertised: 'Public balls to be held during Assize Week in the new Long Room, the biggest in the county.' When the White Hart was to be sold three years later it was described as the finest in Cornwall.

Years before that in 1731, the White Hart had been the home of a remarkable bird. A writer of the time, describing the raven kept by the landlord, said it 'spoke many words as plainly and distinctly as a parrot.' The raven was free to go where it liked and had a younger bird for company, which it was teaching to speak. The will of the innholder at the time, a Mr Neville Barriball, gives us a peep at the treasured possessions of those years. He left his son-in-law a garret of his house, the use only of one bed, one brass crock, six pewter plates and one pewter dish. The son-in-law had no power to dispose of his inheritance, Mr Barriball was certainly giving nothing away.

The hotel's large dining room was formerly the town's Central Assembly Room, the scene of many balls as well as being the occasional theatre. Touring companies would arrive with their acts, their posters announcing such marvels as 'astonishing' rope dancing and the 'surprising forces of Hercules'. Much of the old fabric and charm of this coaching inn and playhouse has been retained, and it is still very much part of Launceston's social scene.

LOOE — *JOLLY SAILOR INN*

The river divides East and West Looe. Both sides look across a harbour where once three-masted double topsail schooners would

The Jolly Sailor at Looe—the sign of a horse on the roof was an indication to smugglers that it was a 'safe house'.

have had to berth two-abreast as they fought for space. On the west bank of the river the Jolly Sailor now stands back a short distance from the water. It was not always so because until land was reclaimed the river used to come up to its door. As the town of Looe is split into two, so is the Jolly Sailor. The low and nautical 500-year-old bar has a Victorian appendage added to the front.

This less commercialised side of the old fishing village once had its smugglers and an old landlady of the Jolly Sailor is famous for having hidden barrels of brandy under her hooped skirts while she denied any knowledge of illicit trade to the customs officers. 'I don't knaw nuthin about it me 'ansums,' would have been the answer to any prying questions in those days. The sign of a horse, which is on the roof of the Jolly Sailor, was an indication to smugglers that it was a 'safe house'. Some of the timbers in the ancient part of the Jolly Sailor are said to have come from ships which sailed with the Armada. The roof is so low in this old bar that in one corner you can see a pit which was dug to enable darts players to throw at the board without hitting the beams. You can see the hooks in the beams which allowed barrels to be raised from tunnels below, said to lead to the harbour so that the illegal comings and goings could not be seen.

LOOE — *SHIP HOTEL*

The Ship in East Looe, is an old inn which has grown into an hotel. On the busier east side of the Looe River, it is in the bustling main thoroughfare in which at least three quite ancient inns survive. Being so close to the harbour it was obviously a favourite hostelry with fishermen, and the occasional smuggler. The main bar has the atmosphere of an old ship, and several Looe characters look at you from the charcoal sketches on the wall.

It was a notable inn over two hundred years ago, with the *Sherborne Mercury* of 1747 noting that debts were to be paid at the house 'known by the sign of the Ship in East Looe'. Thirty years later a ship inventory was held at the Ship. A poster in the bar, dated 1795, shows how the Ship was used as a recruitment centre for the Navy of King George III. Looe men, with their knowledge of the sea, would have been prized recruits on a fighting ship. His Majesty's Commissioners proclaimed that they 'will give the greatest bounty to sixteen landmen or eight seamen who will voluntarily enter themselves to serve in His Majesty's Navy at their rendezvous at the Ship, or at the General Wolfe in Liskeard.'

It was around one hundred years later, in 1888, that the Ship was able to announce that it had finally grown from a small inn to an hotel. The owners proudly boasted: 'The Ship has been enlarged in the past three or four years. It has now three times the accommodation it formerly had.' To find a picture of the Ship in the old days, together with exhibits of Looe's past, go to the Old Guildhall in Market Street, not far from the hotel. This sixteenth-century building houses the town museum, with the old pillory, or stocks, outside for the chastisement of wrongdoers.

LOSTWITHIEL — *MONMOUTH HOTEL*

Lostwithiel is a town full of character and its inns seem to have interesting reasons behind their names. The Monmouth, down in

Devenish
Devenish
MONMOUTH HOTEL
Devenish
Devenish
MONMOUTH
HOTEL
BAR
SNACKS
MORNING
COFFEE
EVENING
MEALS
B & B
ALL ROOMS
FULLY
LICENSED

the valley near the river, is named after a sea battle between the English and the French over two hundred years ago. The interest in the battle, as far as this old town was concerned, lay in the fact that on board the English ship, the *Monmouth*, were many Cornish men, particularly for Lostwithiel as one of the Lieutenants was James Baron second son of the Vicar of Lostwithiel. In her memories of Lostwithiel, published in 1859, Frances M. Hext writes: 'There used to be an old fashioned looking public house called the Monmouth. On the swinging sign over the door was painted the moonlight engagement between the English ship, the *Monmouth*, sixty-four guns, and the French ship, the *Foudroyant*, eighty-four guns, which took place on 28th February, 1758.'

A picture of the battle still graces the entrance to the Monmouth. It is not the 'old fashioned' public house of the past. As Hext writes: 'Within the last few years the old house with its large, roomy, porch has disappeared. In its place has risen up a square plain building.' The Monmouth is in the lower part of Lostwithiel not far from the large Medieval Hall, now called the Old Duchy Palace. It is worth taking a walk around this part of Lostwithiel. Another link with the sea battle can be found at the County Museum at Truro, where a model of the *Foudroyant*, which was presented to Cornish shipowner Richard Chellew, is on display.

The Monmouth Inn has its problem with ghosts. One keeps moving the barrels in the cellar while there is another who pulls flowers out of the vase and throws them on the floor overnight. The Monmouth has certainly stood in Lostwithiel long enough to have a history. In 1823 the inn, stable and brewhouse were to be let, and in 1899 the landlord, as so often happened at the time, was fined for selling adulterated brandy. The Monmouth has survived: ghosts and all.

MORWENSTOW — *BUSH INN*

Morwenstow is Hawker Country.
Robert Stephen Hawker, parson and poet, creator of the Harvest

Left: The Monmouth at Lostwithiel named after a sea battle between the Monmouth *and the* Foudroyant.

MONMOUTH
HOTEL
Devenish

Festival Service and cleric of many parts—a legend in his lifetime
and an even bigger one today—may be dead, but his spirit is alive in
this remote corner of North Cornwall.

'Here,' reflected Sir John Betjeman, 'one is reaching not only the
end of Cornwall but it seems the end of the world.'

Hawker, in the minds of many people, is still about his old parish.

While fellow Bossiney Author Joan Rendell was doing the
research for her book *Hawker Country* several people assured her
perfectly seriously that they believed Mr Hawker haunted the
parish of Morwenstow. 'One elderly lady who lived for many years
in Morwenstow but has now left the parish told me that she had
always felt Hawker's presence in the church during services and she
said that she always felt an urge to glance in the direction of the
spot in the church where Hawker had expressed a wish to be buried.'

'I quite missed him when I left Morwenstow,' she said seriously.
Another lady said quite casually that she had 'often seen Mr
Hawker' walking one of the lanes; she seemed to regard it as a
pleasant meeting with an old friend. 'Several times I encountered
this everyday attitude to what can only be described as a ghost but
which no-one referred to as such. They all spoke as though Mr
Hawker was still a living person,' says Joan Rendell.

Not surprising then to find an inn here with a genuinely haunted
reputation.

The Bush used to boast a fine old thatched roof, but in November
1968 a fire destroyed the lovely roof and roughly half this ancient
inn. Incredibly, today it still generates an old-world atmosphere and
charm.

Jim Gregory, landlord for many years, tells how some people
claimed to have seen a dark shadowy figure moving away from the
blazing building. 'I was assured it wasn't a billow of smoke, it had
too much substance for that . . . I'm not saying it was a spirit or a
ghost but the interesting thing is that we had had lots of strange
happenings up to the date of the fire . . . and it seemed that the fire
killed them off—or almost. Several people claimed to have had
unusual experiences here, and we, ourselves, had heard footsteps
upstairs and on the staircase when we knew there was no-one about
who could possibly make such noises. We had, over the years, a real

Left: The inn sign at the Monmouth.

Landlord Jim Gregory at the Bush Inn at Morwenstow.

floor show of noises, for which there was no rational explanation. For a time we thought the fire had really removed this spirit, but then an American lady guest went to her room and discovered an elderly seafaring character, dressed in old-fashioned clothes. "What are you doing here?" she asked. But without replying, he turned and simply vanished through the wall!'

A clergyman friend of the family who often came to stay was put into the best room in the inn, but, he asked to be moved. 'I feel menaced at night,' he explained. 'I can't sleep in that room.' He saw a shape and felt its presence leaning over the bed.

The Bush Inn, which is a short distance up the narrow road from Morwenstow's clifftop church, has served this farming area for several centuries. It is mentioned in a survey of 1805 and in the mid nineteenth century tithe, or rent, meetings were held here.

In 1859 the landlord was hauled before the local magistrates 'for using considerably defective measures'. You can be sure that does not happen these days.

58

A bush, by the way, is a very old sign for an inn, and Morwenstow's Bush is the only one in Cornwall retaining the name.

MOUSEHOLE — *THE SHIP INN*

This picturesque village, with its narrow streets crammed with tiny granite houses, is also a true working fishing port. Right on the harbour front at Mousehole, or 'Mouzle' to give it its proper local pronunciation, is The Ship Inn with its granite walls looking strong enough to withstand any storm. It will probably surprise most people that this little port was once overrun by foreign invaders. The Spaniards sacked the village in 1595, burning down the homes and buildings, so The Ship dates back to the rebuilding which followed that outrage. It is a charming pub within its hardy exterior,

The Ship Inn at Mousehole—'strong enough to withstand any storm'.

Marconi held meetings at the Old Inn at Mullion.

with open fireplaces and plenty of prints showing Mousehole in the old days.

The night before Christmas Eve Mousehole celebrates Tom Bawcock's Eve, remembering an old fisherman who is said to have saved the village from starvation many years ago when he went out in his boat, after a barren period for the local fleet, and returned with seven sorts of fish. A famous Cornish dish 'Starry Gazey Pie' with fishheads sticking out of the crust is served. Nowhere is this feast celebrated more lustily than The Ship Inn, with the chorus: 'A merry place you may believe, was Mousehole 'pon Tom Bawcock's Eve.'

Another famous resident of the parish who is remembered is Dolly Pentreath, who was buried in nearby Paul Churchyard in 1777. She was one of the last native speakers in the Cornish language. It is possible that one of Dolly's family was once part landlord of The Ship as up to 1849 Messrs Pentreath and Co. together with the Penzance Brewery held the premises on a year-to-year licence.

60

Poet and playwright Dylan Thomas lived at Mousehole before the last war and described it as 'the loveliest village in England'. His love for the place largely stemmed from happy hours in The Ship Inn.

MULLION — *OLD INN*

This pretty thatched Old Inn was probably built at the same time as Mullion's fifteenth-century church. There were once two public houses in tiny Mullion Churchtown but in 1888 the Lord of the Manor, Lord Robartes, thought one was enough so the King's Arms was closed down and the Old Inn stayed in business to continue a cheery welcome both to locals and the many visitors to this lovely part of the Lizard Peninsula.

The sign outside the Old Inn shows Marconi, who sent the first wireless signal across the Atlantic from nearby Poldhu Cove on 12 December 1901. Marconi had sailed to Newfoundland the previous month and heard the morse signal for 'S' being tapped out on the cliffs at Poldhu where he had stayed for some time to build a radio

An earlier view of the Old Inn.

station. Marconi had entered into the social life of West Cornwall during his stay and, although not the sort of man to drop in for a pint at the local, it is understood he held meetings at the Old Inn.

Before Marconi there had been another well-known visitor to the Old Inn. The Reverend Robert Francis Kilvert, whose famous diaries only recently became the subject of a television series due to their unique picture of country life in mid-Victorian times, stayed at the Old Inn in 1870. He drove to Mullion in a large wagonette drawn by a pair of greys. Then the Old Inn was kept by Mary Munday who Kilvert described as 'a genuine Cornish Celt and a good specimen of one—impulsive, warm-hearted, excitable, demonstrative, imaginative, eloquent.' He describes how as he and his companions waited in the sitting room over the stable they heard the horses stomping underneath. The window looked out over a waving field of reddening wheat which grew close up to the wall of the inn.

Mullion is said to be inhabited by people who live long lives, probably because of the temperate weather and the tranquil atmosphere. Certainly the Old Inn has been kept by landlords and families who have had long stays. The Mary Munday referred to in Kilvert's Diaries had been there for some time. In 1810 her brother Samuel, who combined fishing with inn-keeping, had been killed during the launch of a boat. One of his ancestors kept the inn as far back as 1790.

Orlando Bosustow—what a glorious name for a Cornish innkeeper—ran it for 56 years and he was followed by his grandson, David Truscott, who was the licensee from 1946-1979. Much of the furniture was made by him from timber found during years of beachcombing.

The house next to the Old Inn, where Mr Truscott has an antique shop, is called Tavern Coth, Cornish for Old Inn. Inside the inn you will see photographs and information on local wrecks, for the rocks of the Lizard have brought many a vessel to grief. There is also a selection of treasure raised from the wreck of the *Hollandia*, which went down off the Scillies in 1742. This was recovered by the present Old Inn's landlord, Jack Gayton, who was a diver engaged in salvaging from the wreck in the 1970s.

Left: Mr Walter Hicks, founder of the St Austell Brewery, bought the Central Hotel in 1902.

The Central Hotel was previously known as The Commercial.

NEWQUAY — *CENTRAL HOTEL*

Newquay is one of Britain's brightest and busiest holiday resorts, but in the last century it was a quiet fishing port. A guide book of 1859 describes it as 'a small but rising watering hole where the pilchard fishery is pursued on a considerable scale'. Geologists came to Newquay to study the fossiliferous limestone, a few people came for the sandy bays. In the same year, 1859, the premises which now form the Central Hotel were rebuilt, as the name suggests, in the centre of the old town by a Mr William Thomas. He could never have envisaged that the little watering hole was to become one of Britain's most popular holiday resorts.

There had been an inn on the site, believed to be called the Dolphin, since 1755. The property was later called the Ship Inn, then the Old Inn, and at that time included a brew house, stable and three fields. It was a time when Newquay was a smugglers' haunt, when it was not uncommon to see a hundred horses waiting in the dark of night for the arrival of illicit cargo.

Before the inn was rebuilt the leaseholder carried on a cobbler's business in the room above the front arch, while his wife dispensed the liquor downstairs. The front of the inn is as it was when the rebuilding took place, with the original arch above the entrance for coaches. After the rebuilding, it was known as The Commercial and was advertised 'for visitors, families and commercial gentlemen'. It boasted: 'excellent accommodation with home comforts. Special attention and personal superintendence combined with modest charges.'

In 1902 Mr Walter Hicks, founder of the St Austell Brewery, purchased the property for £4,000 and two years later changed the name to the Central Hotel. For 60 years, from 1921, it was run by the Edwards family. After the brewery took over the management, it was extensively renovated.

PADSTOW — *GOLDEN LION HOTEL*

About fifteen minutes before midnight on the eve of the First of May Padstow folk make their way to stand outside the Golden Lion, waiting to hear the strike of midnight, from the church bells. As the last chime fades away they begin to sing, for it is May Day and nowhere is the first day of summer greeted more enthusiastically than Padstow. The singers start with the first verse of Padstow's morning song which begins 'Unite and Unite and let us all unite'. They also have a verse for the landlord and landlady of the Golden Lion, for it is in this old inn that the 'Old Oss' is kept. The night singers go to various parts of the town, without instrumental accompaniment and without the Oss.

There are two Osses in Padstow. The Blue Ribbon Oss appears from the steps of the Institute at 10 a.m. on the morning of May Day, the Old Oss from the Golden Lion an hour later. The celebration welcomes summer and the origins are clouded in the mists of time. It is a custom which was probably widespread in Europe but has died out except for a few areas where old traditions are still valued. Nowhere is it more vigorously and loyally practised and defended than Padstow.

The present Old Oss is of heavy sailcloth, on an elm hoop eighteen feet in circumference. The whiskers on the mask are sheep's wool, and horse-hair is used on the hat and tail. The 'beast' is kept at the Golden Lion, but is not on public display and only comes out on May Day.

The Golden Lion has been an inn for over 200 years. Padstow has many attractions and holidaymakers enjoyed its beauty even before the coming of the now departed railway. In 1798 Padstow was described as 'very convenient for sea bathing, the water being extremely pure, with a sandy bottom, and a commodious bathing machine is kept here for the accommodation of the public'.

The Golden Lion had its own stables and has always been a lively

On May Day in Padstow the Old Oss starts from the Golden Lion.

The Cornish Arms at Pendoggett drawn by Felicity Young of Tintagel.

inn, with Padstonians ready for a song, winter or summer. It also has a proud link with the Padstow Lifeboat, with old posters, pictures and replicas on display.

PENDOGGETT — *CORNISH ARMS*

Pendoggett is on the B3314 road which winds along the North Cornwall coast from Wadebridge towards Tintagel, just one-and-a-half miles inland from the fishing village of Port Isaac. There are some pretty cottages, but the hamlet's most imposing frontage is that of the Cornish Arms.

The exact age of the building is hard to trace but it is probable that both the inn and the surrounding cottages were put up for

Bisquit
FLOWERS
Original
Bitter
FLOWERS

workers in the nearby mines, one of which ran underneath the field on the seaward side of the carpark. Silver, lead, quartz and antimony lie beneath these soils. Modern mineralogists have said there is a viable gold seam in the valley leading down to nearby Port Gaverne, but they do not say what the price per ounce has to reach before it is worth mining.

Like many Cornish pubs, this was once an alehouse brewing its own beer. One old customer's father used to tell the story about a small child who drowned in a beer vat in the corner of the back bar where the beer pump is now situated. This was in the early 1800s, so the Cornish Arms can claim to have been an alehouse since before the Battle of Waterloo. The building itself is older, with parts dating back to 1590 and changing from a cottage to an alehouse when the mines were in full swing. Bedrooms were added in 1956, which transformed it into an inn.

The Cornish Arms now has three roles—as a local pub, a country hotel, and a renowned restaurant. During 1986 it reached its 30th year of continuous opening, night-in night-out, to diners, with the able Gwen Hawken cooking for all but two of the years.

The Cornish Arms must be the only pub in the country to have a clergyman as licensee. The Reverend Alan Wainwright took over the pub on St Valentine's Day in 1978, together with Mr Nigel Pickstone. He had been a vicar in London, Dulwich and Woking before moving to Cornwall, and still stands in when needed for local services. If required he could serve you on your stag night and officiate at your wedding the next day!

An inn with a fine reputation, the Cornish Arms has had some colourful moments in the past. One story tells of the landlady emptying the contents of her and her husband's chamberpots from the bedroom window on some regulars who refused to go home without a drink. It was long after time and she asked them what they wanted. 'Half and half, me dear,' was the reply. Emptying the chamberpots she said: 'Here you are then, half his and half mine.'

Another licensee who was harangued for diluting his scotch said to have pleaded in his defence that he didn't know it was wrong

*Ye Olde Punchbowl & Ladle claims to be the only pub
in Britain with the name.*

because he had always seen his father do it. The Bench doubled the
fine.

Bossiney Books, my publishers, hold their annual authors' lunch
each year here at Pendoggett, and Michael and Sonia Williams, who
run the publishing business from nearby St Teath, have been dining
at The Cornish Arms for twenty-one years.

PENELEWEY, FEOCK — *YE OLDE PUNCHBOWL AND LADLE*

Roses climb around the doors and windows of this picturesque
thatched pub. It stands beside the twisting road which leads to the
King Harry Ferry or to the village of Feock, just off the main route

70

between Truro and Falmouth. Some say it is an eleventh-century inn, but there does not appear to be documentary evidence of this. However, it has certainly had a long association with liquor as it was a customs house before it was granted its licence to sell drinks in the last century. In those days illegal drink and tobacco taken from would-be smugglers was destroyed instead of enjoyed. After the Punchbowl and Ladle was badly damaged by fire in the 1960s the inn had to be rethatched. It was while the thatchers were at work that the builders found a 'bosun's pipe' in the walls. This was a type of furnace, narrowing at one end so that any exploding material would not cause damage while contraband was being destroyed by customs officers. Another such furnace was at Falmouth, where the 'King's Pipe' on Customs House Quay was used for burning up illegally imported cigars, cigarettes and smoking and chewing tobacco.

The building which is now a pub, with three bars, was formerly a small thatched cottage. It has now trebled in size but has lost little of its character. There is a strong aura of the past, with low ceilings, snug corners and old oak beams. After its role as a customs house the building was purchased and converted into an inn by 1890 by Captain William Francis Tremayne. For forty years it was run by the well-remembered Passmore family—Mr and Mrs Bill Passmore and their daughter Queenie. Back in their times it was a real old country pub with no bar. Customers sat around a table and had their drinks brought to them.

The Punchbowl and Ladle claims to be the only one in all Britain with such a name. It is certainly situated in unparalleled countryside, with creeks and country walks all around. The 1940s film version of *Treasure Island* was filmed nearby, with a local beach being used as a tropical island. Many remember the star, Robert Newton, and some of the cast spending some merry nights in the bar of the Punchbowl.

PENRYN — *KING'S ARMS*

The old granite built Borough of Penryn is a most attractive Cornish town with narrow alleys and slate-hung houses. It has a Charter going back to 1265 and was a prosperous town when Falmouth consisted of just a few houses.

Devenish
KINGS
ARMS
KINGS ARMS
Devenish
CAR PARK AT REAR
BED
&
BREAKFAST
ACCOMMODATION
RESTAURANT
John Devenish Potter's
FOOD
AND
GOOD BEER
Grünhalle

In Broad Street—rather a misnomer these days when traffic clogs up its less than ample width—stands the King's Arms, the Borough's oldest inn. The first mention of the King's Arms was in 1489 when an expedition sent by Henry VII to Spain to bring back Katherine of Aragon to marry his son had to put in to the quiet waters of the Fal in rough weather. The party was said to have lodged at the King's Arms.

It was certainly Penryn's premier hostelry. In the 1750s the Bankruptcy Commission used to sit at the King's Arms, and it advertised a good choice with able horses and careful driver. In 1770 the new landlord announced the 'handsome fitting-up of the ancient and accustomed inn', so the King's Arms was of some age even at that time.

The local gentry would meet there and it was obviously a very respectable establishment. According to a newspaper of 1764, the son and heir to Lady Trefusis supped at the King's Arms with his party. It added that a Grand Ball for the ladies was to be held the following Friday. Its respectability is evidenced by the fact that whoever bought the King's Arms also purchased with it a good pew at the Parish Church.

Local Freemasons, regarding themselves as a numerous and respectable lodge, met at the King's Arms even before the 1800s describing it as 'The Principal Inn in this Borough'.

Some people used to say that the nearby Red Lion was older but that establishment was closed by the brewery in January 1985.

Another old pub nearby, the Anchor, came to an ignominious end just a few months later. Drinkers were enjoying their lunch time pints when officials of the local district council walked in to tell them the building was unsafe.

There was not even time for a party to polish off the beer!

PENZANCE — *THE DOLPHIN INN*

If you had stepped outside the front door of The Dolphin 150 years ago or more you would have had the sea-spray right in your face. The Dolphin sits back from the quay, from where the Scillonian sets

Left: The King's Arms at Penryn.

off for those enchanted islands and where fishing boats and small
merchant vessels are moored. But before 1838 the inn was teetering
on the water's edge. Spray, during Cornwall's regular winter gales,
would break right over The Dolphin, and in 1922 it was flooded
during a storm.

The road, which now runs between The Dolphin Inn and the sea,
was made on reclaimed land in 1838 and the high wall, which blocks
the view seawards, was built to protect the inn. The Dolphin, dating
back to the 1540s, plays host to spiritual as well as human customers. The swarthy figure of an old seadog known as Captain
George with his seaman's coat, lace ruffles, brass buttons and tri-
corn hat is said to have a favourite seat by the fireplace in the bar.

In 1873 a nineteen-year-old youth was killed when he fell from a
loft at the back of The Dolphin. He went down a shaft in the middle
of the building, an area which is now used as the bar servery. A fair-
haired figure has been seen in one of the bedrooms, surely the phantom of the young man.

Placed as it was, on the water's edge, it was almost certainly a
haunt for smugglers and some years ago a secret hiding-place was
discovered containing two casks of rum. Dragging noises and the
traces of old-fashioned coarse tobacco are strange phenomena which
are also said to haunt The Dolphin. The notorious hanging Judge
Jeffreys held court in The Dolphin's dining room with prisoners
kept in the cellars so the dragging noise is a haunting reminder of
those brutal days.

Local tradition has it that Sir Walter Raleigh, returning to this
country from an expedition, smoked the first pipe of tobacco at The
Dolphin, so that accounts for the aroma. Sir John Hawkins set up
his headquarters at The Dolphin in 1588 to enlist Cornishmen to
fight the Spanish Armada.

The inn has been host to even more than ghosts, hanging judges
and pipe-smoking adventurers, for in 1868 the landlord was charged
with harbouring loose women. Now, with its old timbers and granite
stone, exposed as it was up to the middle of the last century, The
Dolphin retains character and tradition. It has always been first

74

port of call for fishermen, yachtsmen and sailors, like those days when the quay was just outside the front door and boats were moored up to chains fixed on The Dolphin's wall.

PENZANCE — *TURK'S HEAD INN*

Chapel Street at Penzance still has much of the charm of Cornwall in the seventeenth and eighteenth centuries, with several outstanding buildings, including the Union Hotel, the Egyptian House and old cottages such as those which now form the Admiral Benbow restaurant bars.

Step into the Turk's Head, with its low ceilings and old wood panelling, and you could be going back a century or more. The bar counter is of wood, people sit and chat across a pint in old church pews; the Turk's Head retains the atmosphere of an old seaport pub.

An old seaport pub it most certainly is, for it is reputed to date back to 1233 when, during the Crusades, the Turks came from

Jerusalem to Penzance. It was the first inn in England to be named 'The Turk's Head', others being named at a later date. The original building had a courtyard in the front, which is now the main bar. Alterations were made during the seventeenth century, and the old cellar bar was used by naval ratings when, it is said, there was a tunnel direct to the harbour. This has since been sealed for safety.

The Turk's Head was also a centre of local entertainment over two hundred years ago, when regular concerts were held in the Long Room. What with the theatre and cockpit just up the street at the Union Hotel, the people of Penzance seem to have had a lively time in the eighteenth century.

For some years after 1811 the Turk's Head was kept by Mr Holloway, whose son became a famous pill manufacturer. Thomas Holloway made his fortune and was the founder of Holloway College. With his background he should have invented a pill for hangovers!

The victory at Trafalgar and the death of Nelson was announced from this balcony in the Union Hotel.

A 75-year-old sign inside the Turk's Head at Penzance.

PENZANCE — *UNION HOTEL*

In these days of instant communication, when we hear of events, such as man's first steps on the moon or the conflagration of the Challenger space shuttle as they happen, it is difficult to imagine how news was spread hundreds of years ago. Before the days of radio the news could only travel as fast as transport, be it horse, ship or on foot, could carry it. Because of this, the first news of one of England's greatest sea victories, and the loss of a famous son, Nelson, were first broadcast from the balcony of this Penzance hotel.

On 21 October, 1805, Admiral Lord Nelson took on the French fleet at Trafalgar, off Cadiz in Spain, on a windless sea. The French Admiral, Villeneuve, lost eighteen ships that day, captured or sunk, and that was the end of the striking force of Napoleon's navy. But the British also paid a terrible price, for just after victory was reported to Nelson, he died of his wounds. The British fleet made

sail for home but, heading for Plymouth, they ran into bad weather
and put in to Mount's Bay. An officer from the schooner *Pickle* ran
up to the Union Hotel where there was a banquet in progress
attended by the Mayor of Penzance. It was from the balcony of the
dining room, now called the Trafalgar Room, that victory at
Trafalgar and the death of Nelson was announced.

His death was first officially mourned at the nearby village of
Madron and a banner still kept at the church reads:

> *Mourn for the Brave*
> *The Immortal Nelson's gone*
> *His last Sea Fight is fought*
> *His work of glory done.*

*Billy Herbert of the Norway helps his wife Angela
ashore at Falmouth in 1983 after she had sailed round
the world for charity.*

The Spaniards had attacked the far west of Cornwall over two hundred years previously, in 1595, getting as far as Paul Church. They are said to have set fire to the hotel and the smoke-blackened wall can still be seen today in the Nelson Bar.

In Georgian times the hotel was the centre of life in Penzance, with its Assembly Room, paid for by public subscription, theatre and cockpit. It was certainly lively, with many of the great names of the English Theatre appearing on its stage. As the premier hotel in Penzance during the last century it was one of the great coaching inns until the coming of the railway in 1859. Just across the road from the Union Hotel is one of Cornwall's most unusual shops, Egyptian House, built in 1835.

PERRANARWORTHAL — *NORWAY INN*

The Norway Hotel at Perranarworthal, while standing beside the main Truro to Falmouth road, almost certainly takes its name from the Norwegian ships which brought timber up the estuary. The timber formed the pump rods for the great beam engines which were made at the Perran Foundry, which stands, across the road, as a reminder of this area's industrial past. Now a quiet, sunny valley, it was once a busy river with a large number of men employed at the Foundry, opened in 1791 to make castings for the famous Cornish beam engines which were used to draw water from the mines and which were eventually exported all over the world.

At that time the river was much deeper than it is now and small sailing vessels would discharge their timber at the wharf, just upstream from the Norway.

The pub itself, almost certainly built with some of those Norwegian timbers, was first mentioned in 1829 but probably came into being at the same time as the Foundry. A bridge which borders the front garden of the Norway seems to have been constructed to allow small boats access to the limekiln which can be seen alongside the hotel, while rock from the back garden would have been quarried to construct the Truro Turnpike Road which was opened in 1828. By 1879 the hotel would have looked very much as it does now, with earlier offices and outhouses having been joined together to form the stables and the main bar. Additions were made to the front, now the dining room on the ground floor at the end nearest the limekiln. Large teams of horses from the stables were used to drag the heavy castings from the Foundry to the mines which once abounded in the area.

The landlords of the Norway seem to have been always well regarded. In 1866 the local newspapers reported an accident to Mrs Tresidder, who had lately retired from the Norway. 'Scores of travellers will wish her a speedy recovery' was the comment. Over 100 years later, Angela, the wife of landlord Billy Herbert, sailed around the world for charity, setting off in 1981 and returning in 1983 after having raised £67,000 for cancer care.

A grandmother at that time, Mrs Angela Herbert's daughter Judith had also sailed around the world in 1976. There cannot be another mother and daughter who have completed this remarkable journey.

PORT ISAAC — *GOLDEN LION INN*

Many inns may boast of the connection with smuggling, and in this fishing village you can actually have a drink in a bar near the tunnel where they hid their illicit wares.

The Golden Lion overlooks the busy little harbour at Port Isaac, a picturesque fishing port where in the main street there is only *just* enough room to drive your car.

The pub, which was once known as the Red Lion but seems to have changed colour early in the last century, has one of its bars in the old cellar which used to be used for brewing beer.

The room is known as Bloody Bones Bar, because a body, possibly of a smuggler or fugitive, is reputed to have been found in the tunnel while it was in operation. The entrance to the tunnel is in the old cellar, now used as a store. Planks cover the part of the stone floor where the entrance is to be found, and the tunnel was blocked up many years ago by the customs men.

Bloody Bones Bar, which is only open in the season, leads out to a patio above the beach, with old stables across the yard. Outside here

Right: The Golden Lion at Port Isaac has a smugglers' tunnel which was blocked up by customs men years ago.

80

you really see some of old Port Isaac, a largely unspoilt village of narrow cobbled lanes and slate-hung cottages.

Ale used to be brewed in the cellar and taken upstairs to rooms where fishermen would sit around trestle tables. The bars upstairs are open all the year—still serving those who make their living from the sea.

The inn used to be kept by a well-known fisherman, whose wife would serve the ale while he was at sea. Richard Caesar Cock had moved to Port Isaac from Mevagissey, and after his death in 1818 the inn, then called the Red Lion, was continued for many years by his widow and son.

Richard Cock's will in 1818 shows that he had interests in the fishing industry and a boat named *Old Cornwall.*

RESTRONGUET CREEK, MYLOR —
PANDORA INN

There can be few more pleasant ways to spend a lunchtime than in the sunshine outside this lovely thatched inn, watching the boats sailing on that stretch of river known as the Carrick Roads. Inside, the Pandora has a character acquired over many generations as parts of the building date back to the thirteenth century. As one takes in the maritime scene outside the Pandora, it is hard to imagine that the narrow hill which leads down to it—there is only one road to the Pandora—was once one of the main roads from Falmouth to Truro. Lake's *Parochial History of Cornwall* says: 'a ferry boat was kept here, and the Post Road outside was by much the nearest cut from Falmouth to Truro.'

For hundreds of years boatmen carried passengers across from Restronguet to Feock, cutting miles off the journey by road. A lease of 1789 to Thomas Harvey, a fisherman, granted him the Passage House, the name of the inn at that time, together with the stable and pigs' house. The lease also gave him the right to ferry people across the water 'according to the ancient useage', two boats, oars, ropes and grapples. The journey had its moments of tragedy for in 1791 the ferry boat sank when a horse became restive on the journey across. A Miss Pellow of Penryn and others drowned.

In the same year the inn, by then called The Ship, was bought by

The Pandora was named after the ship that went to search for the survivors of HMS Bounty.

Captain Edwards, who took HMS *Pandora* to search for the survivors of HMS *Bounty*. He ran his ship aground on a reef and was dismissed from the service. Some people say he changed the name of the inn to the Pandora, but it seems more likely that this was done later in the mid nineteenth century by a landlord who saw some publicity value in its connection with a famous chapter of history. The Fal Estuary has been renowned for its seafood, and oyster fishing was a major industry employing many people. The men who gathered this particular delicacy found themselves in trouble after a convivial night at the Pandora in 1920. The court fined a group of oystermen and the licensee of the Pandora for keeping late hours.

*Above: Hurling at St Columb outside the Red Lion
and (right) a tablet outside commemorating a former
landlord James Polkinghorne, champion wrestler.*

ST COLUMB — *RED LION HOTEL*

If we could turn the clock back to be customers standing at the Red
Lion bar in the early years of the last century, we would have been
served by a giant of a man. The innkeeper, James Polkinghorne, had
the neck of a bull, dark curling sideboards, piercing eyes and a deter-
mined jaw. In his prime, James Polkinghorne was a champion
wrestler. No-one is sure of the exact history of Cornish wrestling but
it goes back a long way. At the battle of Agincourt, where banners
depicted the different county contingents, the Cornish one
displayed two wrestlers. Polkinghorne stands as one of the best of

those engaged in this sturdy sport. In his day it was positively brutal, especially when the 'Devonshire style' was employed. The Devonians, wearing boots soaked in bullock's blood and hardened at the fire, hacked at the shins of their opponents who as protection, wrapped bands of hay round their legs below the knee.

There is a tablet on the roadside wall of the Red Lion commemorating Polkinghorne's great match against Abraham Cann, champion of Devon. The match was for £200 a side for the best of three falls. It took place on Tamar Green at Devonport on Monday, 23 October, 1826. Ten thousand people paid over the odds for seats and the hills around swarmed with spectators. Cann, three stone lighter, wore a monstrous pair of shoes, the toes of which had been baked into flints. Polkinghorne, though, struck first, throwing Cann over his shoulder planting him on his back.

'The very earth groaned with the uproar that followed' it was reported at the time. Cornishmen by the hundred jumped into the ring embracing their champion, but the match was not over.

Cann began to kick furiously upsetting the Cornishman's balance, and threw him on his back. The tenth round was contested with absolute fury, and according to the vivid description, some years later, by the Reverend Sabine Baring-Gould, 'Polkinghorne gripped Cann with leonine majesty, lifted him from the earth in his arms, turned him over his head, and dashed him to the ground with stunning force!' The fall was disputed. Polkinghorne was annoyed and left the ring. The match and stakes were awarded to Cann. Everyone wanted to match the two again and various devices were tried. They failed, each had a wholesome dread of the other.

At the time Polkinghorne was landlord of the King's Arms, but he then took over the Red Lion; St Columb's premier inn. It was where the gentry would meet—the *Sherborne Mercury* of 1760 reported that JPs and deputy Lieutenants of Cornwall met at the Red Lion. Balls were held there, and in 1811 a Grand Ball was graced by the presence of the Hon. Louisa Trefusis, the rector's niece. Polkinghorne presided over the inn for twenty years and his son, then granddaughter carried it on until 1884. At the end of the last century, a red lion, taken from a Spanish ship a hundred years before, was given by a naval captain to act as a fitting sign to the inn.

ST COLUMB MAJOR — *RING O' BELLS*

St Columb Major is an old market town, with a Charter dating from the fourteenth century, and where, at the turn of the century, there were at least ten public houses. It is a delightful and very Cornish former 'Rotten Borough' with one narrow street which used to carry all the traffic. Now it is by-passed, but it is well worth turning off to visit this town with its slate-hung houses and a church where there is a thousand year old Celtic cross in the churchyard. The name of the town stems from a sixteenth-century princess, St Columba, who is said to have become a Christian and fled from Ireland to escape the attentions of a pagan prince.

As one leaves St Columb to travel east you see an inn which is said to have its roots in the church but also has some connections

Ring O' Bells, St Columb, built perhaps to house the men who constructed the church tower.

which would bring a frown to the brow of any cleric. The Ring O'
Bells dates back to 1432 as a building and has been a public house
since 1642. It is said to have been built to accommodate the men
who constructed the church tower. They obviously did not carry
every aspect of their religious calling home with them because the
Ring O' Bells is said to have once been a house of ill-repute. It
certainly has had its moments. In 1877 a barmaid was fined by the
local magistrates for throwing boiling water over a customer. Its
connections with the church had a rather macabre outcome in 1858
when a bell hanger working at the church—by the name of Isaac
Pollymountain—hanged himself in one of the bedrooms.

The Ring O' Bells was largely rebuilt in 1857 but it has the atmosphere of an even earlier age. It fits so snugly into St Columb's old
streets and parts of the back of the buildings are typical of the early
eighteen hundreds. It has fared better than another nearby public
house which had a sorry catastrophe in 1872. A fish-seller horse and
cart was backed against the wooden pillars of the Seven Stars.
When the horse began to move the portico of the inn collapsed into
the cart. The horse bolted, and, according to a newspaper of the day,
the landlord was 'stern and wrathful'!

ST IVES — *THE SLOOP INN*

Down in the narrow sun-soaked town of St Ives is one of the great
character waterfront inns of Cornwall: The Sloop. A sloop is an old
and swift sailing vessel, a cutter. This landbound, quaint sloop is
perched by the harbour, full of character, with dark low beams and
superlative views. In 1892 it was described as a 'yellow-washed
house with tiny windows and the snuggest bar parlour imaginable'.
The little state room, with its old-fashioned four-post bedstead
filling it, overlooks the harbour.

In ancient times it was the home of a prominent local family. It
became an inn of some quality and in 1806 a ship sale was held on
the premises. Not all transactions were of such honesty. In 1898 the
Customs men raided The Sloop and the landlady, Mrs Baragwan-
ath, was fined for having smuggled tobacco.

The haunt of fishermen and artists, The Sloop has a number of
paintings on display by various artists including sensitive character
portraits by Hyman Segal, a present-day St Ives artist. There are

also two cartoons by Giles, the famous Fleet Street cartoonist, and a framed poem by the poet Arthur Caddick. There are stories of the pre-Great War years when more than once a painting was presented to the landlord to 'clear the slate'!

The Sloop over the years, must have had some colourful customers: of St Ives characters, Nancy Humphries must rank highly. Nancy, who was noted for many years as supplying the surrounding parishes with fish, had been known to travel more than twenty miles in a day, carrying upwards of a hundredweight of fish on her head. She was clearly a strong woman, but she had a weakness too, as the obituary notice explained in 1826 when Nancy was only 54. 'Her passion for ardent spirits was extreme and its indulgence is supposed to have hastened her end.' Nancy conducted her business in a forthright fashion. If a customer implied that her price for mackerel was a little high, she would reply: 'No, my dea,

*The Sloop Inn at St Ives, perched by the harbour, is
full of character.*

The Burton Brothers at the White Hart, St Teath.

'tedn' no such thing. I do lose 'pon every one I sell: but thanks be, I do sell a perty lot, else I shudden be able to keep my ole man out of the workhouse.'

ST TEATH — *WHITE HART HOTEL*

St Teath, a few miles inland from the North Cornish coast and villages such as Port Isaac and Port Gaverne, was once a busy centre for mining, quarrying and farming. Quarrying for slate at Delabole still continues but now St Teath is more generally thought of as a pleasant spot to retire. The White Hart, which stands in the centre of St Teath, facing the village clock, has seen great changes over the past few hundreds years and has adapted to them. There was an Old White Hart, but St Teath has virtually always been a village with just one pub. The White Hart was mentioned in a survey of 1806 but was largely rebuilt in its present form in 1884. The old kitchen, with its stone oven built into the stone fireplace, is now a snug bar.

In the last century, and in the early part of this, St Teath had two thriving mines, Trewethen-Pengenna and Treburgett, on the outskirts of the village. Metals such as lead-zinc and antimony were brought out of the Cornish soil. The area also had a number of quarries including the famous Delabole Slate Quarry which is over a mile in circumference and is the largest man-made hole in Europe. Back in the old days men would set off early in the morning from St Teath and the surrounding hamlets to walk to the mines and quarries where work was tough and the conditions poor. They were hard days and there was much poverty. Now the mines are derelict and the Delabole Quarry employs fewer people but its slate is still highly prized.

St Teath was the home of a girl who was believed to be a genuine pisky, the little people who haunt the rocks and fields of Cornwall. Anne Jefferies was born in the village in 1626. She performed miraculous cures and people would come for miles to visit her. People said she had been fed for six months by fairies. She would take no money from those she cured and was said to be able to make herself invisible. John Tregeagle, the cruel steward to Lord Robartes, kept her in prison at Bodmin without food because Parliament feared her expressions of loyalty to the King. After three months in Bodmin Jail she was kept under guard at the Mayor's house. During that time she ate no meat but was able to continue with her miraculous cures. Anne Jefferies lived to be over seventy years of age, ending her days as a servant in Devon. Papers written at the time about her remarkable life are kept in the Bodleian Library.

SENNEN near LAND'S END — *FIRST & LAST INN*

Wilkie Collins got it right when he said Land's End is to Cornwall what Jerusalem is to the Holy Land.

Land's End *is* a pilgrimage. The very words fire the imagination.

Sennen, as Arthur Mee put it, 'is next door to Land's End, England's Farthest West and nearest point to America'. The First & Last Inn at Sennen is one of our best known Cornish inns—its

The First & Last at Sennen, 'next door to Land's End'. An early postcard.

very geography ensures that. Times were when it had a notorious reputation with brawls breaking out almost every night. Thought to be built about seven centuries ago, it is unique in that on one side of its inn sign are the words 'The First Inn' and on the other 'The Last Inn in England'.

Some say that in the early part of the 1600s wreckers used the building as their headquarters.

Two formidable ladies ran the inn at different periods, one was Anne Treeve and the other Annie George. This part of Sennen is known as Treeve, named after the former landlady who presided over her inn and wrecking and smuggling operations for more than half a century, the local parson acting as her lieutenant in this illegal 'trade'.

Old newspaper reports confirm that Sennen was notorious smuggling and wrecking territory.

One such report recorded the following: '. . . a crowd of three or four hundred persons attacked the officers of HM Excise who were guarding a quantity of smuggled goods which had been assembled on Sennen beach. The haul included a thousand gallons of brandy, a similar quantity of rum, five hundred pounds of tobacco and other spoils . . .'

A complicated case, reported in great detail, it went on to say:
'The principal witness for the prosecution was a certain Annie
George who, until a short time before had been the keeper of the
Sennen Inn, a place with a reputation of being the resort of all the
idle blackguards in the county : . .' Her husband Joseph George was
further stated to have been '. . . the smuggling agent for his land-
lord, a well-to-do farmer of Sennen Parish named as Dionysius
Williams . . .'

Because of his knowledge of the landlord's illicit trade, George de-
faulted in his rent to Williams who unwisely decided to eject the
Georges from the inn. The threat so infuriated Annie that she
turned King's evidence against Williams who was sentenced to a
long period in jail.

The inn has also had fine recommendations from some writers.
The Reverend J. Sweete, on a tour of 1777—all the clergy of that
time seemed to have some excuse for a tour—wrote: 'We ordered a
jug of beer, which really was as good as any we met with throughout
our whole journey.'

However, eighteen years later in 1795 another traveller wrote of
the First and Last: '. . . the best way is to take your dinner with you.
They have only fish and sometimes not even that. We took with us a
couple of roasted chickens and a tongue, some rolls and a bottle of
red port.'

I wonder what a modern landlord would make of a family who
walked into his premises with that sort of feast!

Landlords and landladies of the inn have managed to make a good
living. It was reported in 1867: 'The proprietor of the famous First
and Last Inn in England has built a new hotel at Land's End.'

STRATTON — *TREE INN*

The Tree Inn, parts of which date to the thirteenth century, was
formerly the manor house of the Grenvilles, a family famed and
revered in Cornwall. However, although the Grenvilles certainly
made their mark in both Cornish and British history, it was one of
their servants who has become a genuine giant of Cornish folklore.

Anthony Payne, son of a tenant farmer, was born in the manor
house, Stratton, now the Tree Inn. His date of birth was not recorded, but he rapidly rose to immense size and strength. It was

*Above: The Tree Inn at Stratton where Anthony
Payne (left), the Cornish Giant, was born.*

said that he was such a huge boy that his school mates used to work
out their arithmetic lessons in chalk on his back. At 21 he was taken
into the establishment of the Grenvilles original mansion at Stowe.
His strength became a legend in the area. Seven feet two in height
without his shoes at 21, he grew another 2 inches. He was not tall and
lanky, but stout and well proportioned in every way. He performed
remarkable exhibitions of strength, on one Christmas Eve bringing
in an ass across his shoulders and a boy with faggots for the fire into
the great hall at Stowe.

During the Civil War Cornwall was behind the King, Charles I.
The great battle of Stamford Hill was fought on 16 May 1643 near
Stratton. The Royalist soldiers were outnumbered, but Anthony
Payne, mounted on his sturdy cob Sampson, rallied his troops and
terrorised the enemy into fleeing.

However, at the next pitched battle near Bath the forces of the King were defeated and Payne's proud master, Sir Beville Grenville, was killed. Payne had led on the Grenville troops to the fight, having mounted John Grenville, a youth of sixteen, on his father's horse to continue the battle.

At the Restoration Sir John Grenville was created Earl of Bath. Payne, held in great favour by the King, was made yeoman of his guards.

After his death at the Tree Inn, where he had been born, neither door nor stairs was big enough for the huge coffin containing Payne's remains to be carried out. The joists had to be sawn through and the floor lowered with rope and pulley to enable the giant to pass out to his last resting place under the south wall of Stratton Church. The room where he died is above the present public bar and there is an imprint in the ceiling where they had to cut through.

An interesting aside is a story of Payne's portrait which is now in the County Museum at Truro. Payne was painted by Kneller, but when Stowe Manor was dismantled the picture was removed to Penheale, another Cornish residence of the Grenville family. The portrait was not valued and was soon forgotten. A Cornish historian named Gilbert, whilst staying at an old inn in Launceston, heard about the painting and went to Penheale, where the farmer's wife said they possessed 'a carpet with the effigy of a large man on it', that had been given to her husband by the steward on the estate. It was rolled up and dirty, and she gladly sold it to C. S. Gilbert for £8. On Gilbert's death his effects were sold at Devonport for £42. In London it was recognised as the work of Kneller and resold for £800. It was eventually bought by Sir Robert Harvey and presented to the Royal Institution of Cornwall. Go and see this portrait of a giant of a man at the Truro Museum.

The Tree Inn is an historic building with a fascinating past. The low ceiling of the restaurant is beamed with timbers from ships wrecked off the Cornish coast. It was a coaching inn, and in 1779 the Exeter Flying Post carried an advertisement announcing good new beds at the Tree with good stalls, stables and sheds.

One landlord was a devotee of a noble Cornish art. In 1828 it was reported that Mr Lyle of the Tree would spare no expense in obtaining good men for Stratton wrestling. A few years earlier a man had

The Mill House at Trebarwith—AA Inn of the Year in 1985.

been hanged for a theft at the Tree on Stratton Fair Day. An advertisement in the *Royal Cornwall Gazette* of 1875 stated: 'To let: one of the oldest commercial and posting houses in the West of England.' Who would argue?

TREBARWITH near TINTAGEL —
THE MILL HOUSE INN

The Mill House, which achieved national recognition as the AA Inn of the Year in 1985, is an old building with a relatively new role.

Situated in the bottom of the valley which leads down to the rugged Trebarwith Strand, it is approached by steep and narrow roads from either Tintagel or Delabole.

As its name suggests, this inn of stone and slate used to be a corn mill. The building dates back to the seventeenth century, with the present dining room the oldest part. This, together with the lounge, was part of the original miller's cottage. The mill pond was further up the valley, and the leats and slurries leading to the mill can still be seen. An axle from the overshot wheel which was used to provide the power to grind the corn goes through the wall of the building, and some of the crushing wheels lie in the grounds of the inn. An old hoist, to haul up sacks of corn is still there.

The mill was in use up to the Second World War, with the Boney family in occupation. After the war Mr Fred Whiting saw the old millhouse, with no bathrooms or electricity, and with his wife bought it and started to convert it in order to take in guests. They started with brass bedsteads, oil lamps and candles, and people slept in bedrooms where the old grinding stones used to be.

The building got a licence as a pub in 1959 when the bottom part was converted into a bar, and the Whitings sold the property in 1974.

Good victuals and atmosphere led to it eventually winning the AA title and other awards.

Once this valley was alive with miners, quarrymen and, of course, the miller. It still has an atmosphere of the past.

TREEN — *LOGAN ROCK INN*

The cliffs at Treen, not far from Land's End, are well worth a visit—but make sure you have your walking shoes. The village, un-spoilt granite cottages looking as though they have been carved out of the nearby cliffs and transported to a more sheltered bank inland, has a pub whose name comes from a nearby large stone which was the centre of a great local controversy early in the last century.

The sign outside Logan Rock public house will give you a clue to the story. It pictures a naval officer pushing a huge granite stone.

The rock, which crowns a headland which has a succession of natural piles of granite tors, was famous as a 'logging stone', logging being the local word for rocking. Weighing about ninety tons it was so exactly poised upon one point that anyone, by applying his shoulder to it, could make the whole mass rock. In a high wind it could be seen rolling on its pivot. Local people, who

*The Logan Rock Inn is named after a rocking stone
on the cliffs which was dislodged by a young naval
officer to everyone's consternation.*

would proudly take visitors to the stone via fields from the village,
boasted that no man could throw the Logan Rock from its balance.

This stirred up a challenge in a silly lieutenant, Hugh Goldsmith,
of the cutter HMS *Nimble* which was off Land's End looking for
smugglers in 1824. He decided to do what was said to be the imposs-
ible. With fourteen of his men, Lieutenant Goldsmith, using hand-
spikes and a handscrew, threw over the stone. There was uproar.
Two poor families in Treen whose livelihood came from attending
visitors to the stone, were deprived of their means of support. The
whole of Cornwall was roused; fishermen threatened the life of the
perpetrator Goldsmith, and Magistrates were summoned to con-
sider what could be done.

The Admiralty ordered Lieutenant Goldsmith to restore the
Logan Rock to its old position, at his own cost, or forfeit his commission. Luckily for Goldsmith the stone had not rolled into the sea,
but was stuck in a cleft in the rocks. On 2 November 1824, in the

*The Wheel Inn at Tresillian in earlier days. Lord
Fairfax signed a treaty here in 1646.*

presence of vast crowds, ladies waving their handkerchieves and
men letting off fireworks, the ninety ton block was raised back in
position. It was no longer so perfectly balanced as before, but it
'logged' well enough to satisfy the crowds. Prints showing how the
feat was performed, and a copy of the bill for the job, about £130,
can be seen in the bar of the Logan Rock.

The inn itself is believed to be around 400 years old, and with its
low beamed ceilings and granite fireplaces it must be very much as
it was when people called in for refreshment on their way to watch
Goldsmith's feat. The present bar used to be the living accommodation while drinks were served in jugs across the covered passage-
way in what is now the family room. The inn, together with surrounding cliffland was given to the National Trust in the 1930s.

Some of the local people sit on an old mule chest which is inside a
disused granite fireplace in the bar. When the landlord tried to re-
place it with a proper seat there was an outcry—shades of the saga
of the Logan Rock.

TRESILLIAN — *THE WHEEL INN*

Cornwall was a Royalist stronghold in the Civil War of 1642 to 1646, and men of the county quickly joined the Army of the West under Sir Ralph Hopton, who had brought his 160 cavalrymen from Dorset.

There were battles at many towns in Cornwall, most notably Stratton and Lostwithiel, but if you travel through the village of Tresillian, just east of Truro, you will pass the spot where a peace treaty was signed.

Tresillian, in the warmth of a sunny day, is the sort of lazy riverside spot where anyone would have to stop fighting, and The Wheel Inn, with its thatched roof and garden beside the River Fal is the place to come to peace with the world. The Wheel Inn is where Lord Fairfax, the Parliamentary General, made his headquarters during the signing of a peace treaty in 1646, while his entourage were housed in the surrounding cottages.

The Wheel Inn today—
its sign in thatch in the roof.

The hamlet was then known as Tresillian Bridge. A plaque commemorating the signing of the treaty is affixed to the Sunday School opposite Tresillian Church—many say it should be hanging above The Wheel Inn. The plaque reads 'To the memory of all brave Cornishmen who died in the great Civil War 1642-1646'. Near the bridge was arranged, on Tuesday, March 10, 1646, the Cessation which led to the Treaty of Surrender signed four days later in Truro, and the end of hostilities in the West.

A ship's wheel appears in thatch on the roof of The Wheel, an appropriate symbol for an inn with a river on one side and a road on the other.

Some years ago an old sign was found in The Wheel, saying:

> *Be merry friends, enjoy your beer,*
> *but do not swear or gamble here.*

In 1893 the landlord, a character named Hiram Pearse, whose descendants still remember him with affection, was fined by Truro Magistrates for allowing gambling at skittles. I wonder if he had the sign made to warn his customers that he was anxious to avoid another appearance before the bench.

TRURO — *THE ROYAL HOTEL*

Truro, as the administrative centre of Cornwall, has seen much development and its numerous taverns, inns, hotels and beerhouses, have made way to so-called 'progress' over the years. The greatest loss was the old Red Lion, the former house of the Foot family, which was demolished after a runaway lorry had made it unsafe.

However, even in the early days of the Red Lion as an inn and tavern, the foremost coaching house was The Royal Hotel, which had a variety of names before its present title. It was regal from the start. The present hotel was built around 1800 and known as the King's Head, being constructed in the garden of an older pub of the

Left: The Royal Hotel acquired its name after a visit to Truro in 1846 by Prince Albert.

same name which dates back another 100 years. The change of site was to make possible the building of Truro's Lemon Street.

In 1804, when described as newly erected, the King's Head was in the news when a reward of 20 guineas, quite a handsome sum at the time, was offered for information against the person who had broken many of the windows. It then became Pearce's Hotel, after the owner William Pearce, who had moved from Redruth. He was obviously impressed with the inventiveness of his fellow townsman, Richard Murdoch, because the hotel then took the very modern step of being lit by gas. The name 'The Royal Hotel' came about in 1846

after Prince Albert visited Truro. Mr Pearce was given permission
to prefix 'Royal' to the hotel sign and he also placed a large terra-
cotta sign over the door. After Pearce came Robert Dobell, who was
landlord for 22 years and whose name lives on as the title of one of
the bars.

The Royal's link with coaching is shown in 1872 when the former
host of the hotel died. Mr Alfred Tedder, the former driver of the
Brighton coach when the Great Western ended at Plymouth, had
taken on the working of the Cornish mails. The Royal has many
references to its own history and local events displayed in one of the
bars underlining how it has been part of the life in Truro over many
generations.

WADEBRIDGE — *MOLESWORTH ARMS HOTEL*

Gone are the sailing ships. Even in this century, they sailed up to
Wadebridge. You can still see the ancient wharves and quays below
the bridge. 'When the tide is out,' Arthur Norway wrote of Wadebridge, 'it is as though the town has lost its soul.'

Molesworth Street is the town's main thoroughfare. Here stands
the Molesworth Arms, one of the most interesting buildings in
Wadebridge, a sixteenth-century inn with a ghostly legend. Tra-
ditionally a phantom coach, drawn by four horses, and driven by a
headless coachman, careers through the courtyard at midnight on
New Year's Eve.

Outside any legendary claim, there have been several inexplicable
happenings upstairs at the Molesworth Arms: the ringing of a bell
in an empty room, the invisible yet audible rustle of skirts on the
stairs leading to the attic, the strange slamming of a door by unseen
hands—these are linked to the murder of a woman in the drawing
room whose body was dragged to the attic. Fact or fiction? There is
certainly a dark stain beneath the carpet on that angled floor of the
drawing room. The first floor of the Molesworth, in places, gives the
feeling of being aboard ship in a heavy swell. The ground and first

floors are connected by a lovely curved wooden staircase. First known as The Fox, later rechristened The King's Arms and then The Fountain, it was in 1817 that the landlord John Stephens gave the inn its present name in respect of the family who lived on the other side of the river at Pencarrow. The Molesworths, who once owned the building, were the principal landowners hereabouts, and the family crest is over the main entrance, while in the entrance hall hangs a picture of the Rt Hon. Sir William Molesworth, Bart, a former Member of Parliament and Secretary of State for the Colonies.

Early in the last century winter concerts and balls were held at the Molesworth.

A tribute to the comfort and atmosphere of the premises, written in *The West Briton* of 1869 could well apply today. The writer told his readers: 'when the glasses are full, and the pipes smoking all round the long table in the Molesworth Arms Hotel, it is a thorough picture of animal enjoyment.'

ZENNOR — *THE TINNERS' ARMS*

The coastal road from St Ives westward towards Land's End takes you through some never-to-be-forgotten countryside.

It twists, rises and falls through a combined grandeur of moor and cliffs, sea and sky. There are huge granite boulders among the heather, but trees are scarce in a landscape which can feel the full wrath of an Atlantic storm.

The road and tors descend to Zennor Churchtown, where The Tinners Arms stands opposite the partly Norman church.

Parts of The Tinners are thought to date to the thirteenth century, and the premises could have been put up to house the men who built the church. The design of the first floor has led people to believe it was a meeting place, with space for cattle below.

The Tinners, now the only inn of that name in a county renowned for its miners, has just one rectangular bar, with sturdy granite walls over two feet thick and a fireplace at each end.

Left: The portrait of the Rt Hon. Sir William
Molesworth hanging in the entrance hall of the hotel.

*The Tinners' Arms at Zennor—'the only inn of that
name in a county renowned for its miners'.*

It has certainly been known as The Tinners for nearly 200 years,
and had a rough and ready history in the last century when miners
would take on anyone after having one too many.

In April 1886 the landlord, William Nankervis, was charged by
the local magistrates with keeping late hours. He escaped with a
light fine after explaining that he went by the Zennor church clock,
not GMT.

If you go in the church you will see a mermaid carved on one of the
fifteenth-century bench ends. The legend of the Mermaid of Zennor

has it that the son of a former squire had such a beautiful voice that his singing in the church drew a mermaid up from the deep to hear him. She sat in church Sunday after Sunday until the·young man, entranced by her beauty, followed her down the cliffs to the sea and was never seen again.

The writer D. H. Lawrence, who lived nearby for part of the 1914-18 War, was a customer at The Tinners, but not a popular one. Over a pint he was inclined to speak out against the war, and did nothing to conceal his loathing of the Lloyd George government. Worst of all, he and his wife, Frieda, the daughter of a Prussian Baron, sang German songs loudly and defiantly.

In August 1917 a German submarine was sighted off the coast near Zennor. Destroyers and planes hurried to the spot, and a slick

Zennor—looking down on church and inn from the rock where Wesley preached.

of black oil on the water appeared, showing that one charge, at least, had found its target. Allegations grew—lights signalling out to sea at night—and one day Frieda was halted by a coastguard, who feeling her rucksack, declared: 'Ah, a camera!' Frieda instead produced a loaf of bread, but gossip and suspicion were spreading.

The Lawrences' mail was withheld and scrutinised. Later soldiers searched the cottage in their absence and finally a posse appeared consisting of a young Army officer, the friendly local policeman, and two detectives. The contents of every cupboard and drawer were examined and a notebook of Lawrence's concerning his Nottingham days was confiscated. The young officer set seal on the visit by presenting an expulsion order: the Lawrences were to leave Cornwall within three days and without explanation.

'And that's what you call English justice!' hissed Frieda.

It was—and in 1917 it was Cornish justice too.

A more recent customer of note at The Tinners Arms was Lord Hunt of Everest fame. The cliffs hereabouts were used for climbing—the schooling ground of mountaineers.

Also Available

HISTORIC INNS OF DEVON
by Monica Wyatt
The author visits 50 famous hostelries scattered over the county.
'Monica Wyatt's writing is pitched at just the right level . . . thoroughly researched, shot through with real enthusiasm and never donnish. She shares her discoveries with you . . . I raise my glass.'

The Western Evening Herald

COASTLINE OF CORNWALL
by Ken Duxbury
Over 100 illustrations including 45 in colour.
Ken Duxbury has spent thirty years sailing the seas of Cornwall, walking its cliff-tops, exploring its caves and beaches, using its harbours and creeks.
'. . . has used his unique experience of his years of sailing around Cornwall . . .'

Cornish Scene

THE MOORS OF CORNWALL
by Michael Williams
Contains 77 photographs and drawings. The first ever publication to incorporate the three main moorland areas of Cornwall.
'As well as photographs the work is illustrated by the delightful sketches of Felicity Young. In all a splendid evocation of the Cornish Moors.'

Dr James Whetter, The Cornish Banner

PEOPLE AND PLACES IN CORNWALL
by Michael Williams
Featuring Sir John Betjeman, Marika Hanbury Tenison, Barbara Hepworth and seven other characters, all of whom contributed richly to the Cornish scene.
'. . . outlines ten notable characters . . . whose lives and work have been influenced by "Cornwall's genius to fire creativity" . . . a fascinating study.'

The Cornish Guardian

HEALING, HARMONY & HEALTH
by Barney Camfield
Healing in its various forms, the significance of handwriting and dreams, and psycho-expansion.
'If you are tuned in to the right wave length of new age thinking . . . you won't want to put it down until you get to the last page.'

David Rose, Western Evening Herald

WESTCOUNTRY MYSTERIES
Introduced by Colin Wilson
A team of authors probe mysterious happenings in Somerset, Devon and Cornwall. Drawings and photographs all add to the mysterious content.
'. . . unresolved stories from past and present. Most beguiling is David Foot's essay on Thomas Shoel, the 18th century composer from Somerset. I would buy the book for that story alone . . .'

Margaret Smith, Express and Echo

PEOPLE & PLACES IN DEVON
by Monica Wyatt
Dame Agatha Christie, Sir Francis Chichester, Dr David Owen, Prince Charles and others. Monica Wyatt writes about eleven famous people who have contributed richly to the Devon scene.
'A very interesting title from this rapidly expanding publishing house. Indeed, for a "cottage" industry it's going from strength to strength, its territory now covering an area from Bristol to Land's End.'
Irene Roberts, The South Hams Newspapers

MYSTERIES IN THE DEVON LANDSCAPE
by Hilary Wreford & Michael Williams
Outstanding photographs and illuminating text about eerie aspects of Devon. Seen on TSW and Channel 4. Author interviews on DevonAir and BBC Radio Devon.
'A Devonian and a Cornishman have combined to produce a pictorial account of a journey . . . Using their imagination and curiosity, the authors found themselves drawn by the magnetism of the strange shapes that people the Devon landscape.'
The Book Exchange, International Monthly Book Review Journal

SEA STORIES OF CORNWALL
by Ken Duxbury. 43 photographs
'This is a tapestry of true tales', writes the author, 'by no means all of them disasters—which portray something of the spirit, the humour, the tragedy, and the enchantment, that is the lot of we who know the sea.'
'Ken is a sailor, and these stories are written with a close understanding and feel for the incidents.'
James Mildren, The Western Morning News

SUPERNATURAL IN SOMERSET
by Rosemary Clinch
Atmospheres, healing, dowsing, fork-bending and strange encounters are only some of the subjects featured inside these pages. A book, destined to entertain and enlighten—one which will trigger discussion—certain to be applauded and attacked.
'. . . an illustrated study of strange encounters and extraordinary powers in people and nature . . .'
Somerset County Gazette

MYSTERIES IN THE SOMERSET LANDSCAPE
by Sally Jones
Sally Jones, in her fourth Bossiney title, travels among the Mysteries in the Somerset Landscape. An intriguing journey among deep mysteries in a 'fascinating and varied landscape'.
'This is a whirlwind package holiday of sorcery and legend, touching down here and there before whizzing off in search of still more fascinating fare.'
Mid Somerset Series of Newspapers

We shall be pleased to send you our catalogue giving full details of our growing list of titles for Devon, Cornwall and Somerset and forthcoming publications.
If you have difficulty in obtaining our titles, write direct to Bossiney Books, Land's End, St Teath, Bodmin, Cornwall.